A WORLD OF
DIFFERENCE
THE BIG GREEN

CW01567110

Recycle, Recycle, Recycle! Love the world you live in. Be good to your planet. Don't be mean, be green! Recycle, Recycle, Recycle!

Verses From The West Midlands

Edited by Lisa Adlam

First published in Great Britain in 2009 by:

 Young**Writers**

Young Writers
Remus House
Coltsfoot Drive
Peterborough
PE2 9JX
Telephone: 01733 890066
Website: www.youngwriters.co.uk

Foreword

Young Writers' A World of Difference is a showcase for our nation's most brilliant young poets to share their thoughts, hopes and fears for the planet they call home.

Young Writers was established in 1990 to nurture creativity in our children and young adults, to give them an interest in poetry and an outlet to express themselves. Seeing their work in print will encourage them to keep writing as they grow, and become our poets of tomorrow.

Selecting the poems has been challenging and immensely rewarding. The effort and imagination invested by these young writers makes their poems a pleasure to enjoy reading time and time again.

Contents

The Poems

Go Green

What will become of our world?
I really dread to think
Not so many fields and trees
As they are slowly chopped away
What will become of our world?
I really dread to think.

What will become of our world?
I really dread to think
Let's cut down on our waste
And recycle where we can
Replace our bulbs with energy bulbs
But flick the switch to off
Then we are doing our bit
What will become of our world?
I really dread to think.

What will become of our world?
I really dread to think
Do we really need to go out in our car or couldn't we walk?
Let's all do our bit by washing at 30 degrees
Which will really help to go green
And let's just keep everything in the world
Just how it should be
Let's go green
What will become of our world?
I really dread to think.

Amy Humpage (11)
Alderman Smith School

Green Poem

Stop the litter, it's too bitter
Stop the pollution, find a solution
Throw your tin, in that red bin
Help the homeless, stop being so hopeless
Be more able to invest all, to be successful
Let's stop the racism and save the world!

Aston Dowsett (11)
Alderman Smith School

Being Homeless

I get up in the morning
Not having had much sleep
Not eaten anything for days
I'm feeling weak
Pack up my belongings
It doesn't take much time
As everything around me
Isn't really mine
Looking through shop windows
And taking in the views
Wishing I was one of them
Waiting in the queues
I wish I could be treated
With kindness, love and care
But most people just walk past
But some stop to stare
Walking through parks and alleys
Finding anywhere to roam
Not knowing if I'll ever go into
A cosy, warm home.

Hadley Macaulay (12)
Alderman Smith School

Make The World Litter Free

Litter, litter,
It is so bitter,
Why do we,
Have to see,
It all over the floor,
But not on the door.

Litter, litter,
It is so bad,
It makes me so sad,
Most people think,
They can drink
And drop it on the floor.

Seraiah Morgan (12)
Alderman Smith School

Home No More

I had a home once, it was great, you see,
It was warm and cosy and perfect for me,
Now I'm here and I'm stuck in a bush,
People stare and past me they rush.
They make me feel more worthless each day,
All I can do is sit and pray,
Pray for some money, pray for a home,
Pray for someone to give me a comb,
I look like a wreck, my hair needs a cut,
If I could afford it, then I'd get off my butt.

My shoes are tattered, my clothes are ripped,
I need some help; need to get a grip,
It's freezing cold and I'm soaking through,
Looking forward to summer, at least the sky's blue.
It's getting late now and darker than night,
My stomach is churning, my head full of fright,
I look up to Heaven and what can I see,
But a dark, gloomy sky and the reflection of me.

Siobhan Stain (14)
Alderman Smith School

Litter

I was walking down the street one day
To see if my friends would come and play
I saw her drop rubbish on the path
'What is this?' I asked
So I followed her to her door
I asked her, 'Why's this rubbish on the floor?
It's called litter, haven't you heard?
It's hurting some cats and birds
They get it stuck around their necks
Which can also kill our animals and pets
We love our animals very much,
But they wouldn't be there to care for and touch
So I hope this has helped you to learn,
Don't drop litter, save our Earth!'

Sarah Timms (13)
Alderman Smith School

3

Environment, Environment

Environment, environment
Look after the environment
What can we do?
What can we do?
You could recycle
There are lots that can be recycled
Even a shoe!
Environment, environment
What can we do?
What can we do?
Pick up litter
You might save £1.20
For a pint of bitter!
Environment, environment
Look at the environment
Do you want it to be
Like this in ten years time?
Think and read my rhyme!

Rachel Victoria Beveridge (12)
Alderman Smith School

It Is Not Fair

Being homeless, it's not fair
All they do is stop and stare
Sitting on the ground, alone
No one can hear me moan
I cannot afford clothes
I have no one, it's just me
And my cardboard box
It's not fair, I am upset
I am in £5,000 worth of debt
I don't have breakfast
I don't have lunch
When everyone else can have brunch
When I cannot even have a munch.

Ashley Hill (13)
Alderman Smith School

Litter, Litter

Litter, litter, all around,
Living, breathing, on the ground,
People don't care anymore,
Whether it's in the bin or on the floor.

Wrappers floating on the lake,
Dirty cigarette packets, whatever make,
People think it's a funny joke,
To sit and watch the birds choke.

Plastic bottles here, metal cans there,
Morrisons and Asda bags everywhere,
Chip shop wrappers litter the road,
Dirty nappies by the load.

The place is a mess
And people won't confess,
To dropping litter on the floor
And polluting the Earth even more.

Sarah Faulconbridge (12)
Alderman Smith School

Green

Green, green and green,
I want a holiday with a scene,
Of green, green and green,
A summer of green, green and green trees,
A landscape of green grass,
A view full of green vegetables,
The colour green is a beauty that must be seen!
From a moving vehicle screen,
And while we hold onto all these machines,
That deprive us of the colour green:
So for green, green and green,
I will travel continents across and in-between
And also to any place that I have never been,
I will make it routine, just to see,
Green, green and green!

Leah Bacciochi-Langston (11)
Alderman Smith School

Litter, Litter, Everywhere

Litter, litter, everywhere
But not a drop in the bin
If everyone didn't care
And didn't put the rubbish in

Losing lottery tickets, beer cans
Remains of cigarettes, chewing gum on the floor
More rubbish chucked out by cars and vans
Part of our city tour

Why can't people walk a couple of paces
To get to the bin, or put the rubbish in their pockets
And put the junk in the trash when they get to their places
It isn't as complicated as making a rocket!

Rubbish doesn't look nice
It gives you a frown
It attracts rats and mice
So drive it out of town!

Jordan Marlowe (14)
Alderman Smith School

Litter

Litter, litter, is really bad
Sometimes it makes me feel sad
Then it can meet
You in the street
Sometimes you can see it
In your sleep
People just drop it anywhere
Do they think? Do they care?
Litter, litter, everywhere
Put it in the bin
And show you care
Make our world a tidy place
Just by not making that big mistake
Bin your litter to show you care
I do, do you care?

Amy Richards (12)
Alderman Smith School

Litter

Litter is bad
It makes me feel sad
To see it all
Over the place

In some spots
Paper is dropped
It gets wet
And makes a mess

A carrier bag is dropped
When you go to the shop
You stop
Before you drop

I wish I could see this stop
And people would do a swap
And bin all their litter
Or take it home with them.

Sophie Bastock (12)
Alderman Smith School

On The Street

On the street,
So hungry,
So cold,
With nothing to eat.

There is no home,
Only the street,
So really sad,
It's bad.

The sadness in the air,
So hard to bare,
They cry every night,
It's quite a fright.

Bethan Pegg (12)
Alderman Smith School

Poem On War

I can't go to bed,
'Cause the things in my head,
Make it hard to sleep,
Oh dear, what am I going to do?

It's like it happened today
And it won't go away,
Don't ask me to try and count sheep.

It's a part of the past,
They say memories won't last,
But with me it's going to last.

When you're lying in your bed,
Try and sleep it off,
But only if you remember,
The war is now over.

Rachel Keenan (14)
Alderman Smith School

What Could It Be?

There is a beautiful place
But what could it be?
Not many people talk about it
It's like it's locked up in a case.

It's getting disturbed by pollution
What could it be?
If people cared
Then there would be a solution.

The trees are disappearing
But what could it be?
More and more of them choppers are appearing
But what could it be?

Abigail Proctor (12)
Alderman Smith School

Green Poem

We are the young generation,
We learn about the environment in our education,
We need to find a solution,
To stop the amount of pollution,
We started to recycle at home,
From baked bean tins to our mobile phone,
The exhaust on our cars pollutes the air,
So why don't we walk or car share?
All the ice is melting, who cares?
I know the penguins do and the polar bears!
If we could all make a contribution,
We would be closer to finding our solution!

Ben Woods (11)
Alderman Smith School

Being Homeless

Being homeless is so sad,
Why does it have to be bad?
I'm so hungry, I'm so cold,
All I want is someone to hold.

Here at night, with drunk people about,
Acting like a silly sprout,
Here, there and everywhere,
People turn to laugh and stare.

Being homeless is so sad,
Why does it have to be bad?

Natalie Goodwin (14)
Alderman Smith School

Homeless

I sit here in the blistering cold
With no one to love and no one to hold
My mummy left me with no protective ceiling
I told her, I don't believe in you, I don't know what I'm feeling
I thought there was someone down there, down there deep
I thought I was going to wake up, but my alarm didn't beep
Instead of being here alone
I just want a family of my own
One day, I hope that will come true
Mum, I love you!

Hollie Timms (12)
Alderman Smith School

Be Green!

Butane gases and the ozone layer,
Don't recycle and you're the betrayer,
Use your red boxes
And save the foxes!
Save our planet!
Our carbon footprint needs to be reduced,
Less cans will have to be produced!
Petrol is the gas that smells so rotten,
Soon our world will be forgotten!

Daniel Southall (12)
Alderman Smith School

A Green Life

You must be kind to all living things,
Do not think of just yourself, think of the homeless,
Become green and don't be mean,
So reduce, reuse and recycle,
So soon you will be as green as the grass,
Don't litter, be clean and soon you will gleam!

George Bowman (11)
Alderman Smith School

Let's Be Fair

No more mean, it's good to be green
It's bad to litter because it's bitter
We need to think more of rainforests
And be considerate of animals
They are a big part of our natural world
Why be at war? It only hurts more
Racism is not fair, everyone is equal
Everyone has a talent
Which is what makes our world balance.

Shannon Delaney (11)
Alderman Smith School

The White House

The outside was a mask
For what happening inside
The screams that were heard
No one could hide!

The blood, the noise and the screams
Of which we'll never forget
For they will stay in our dreams
Until the very end!

Jess Wigley, Annalise Hill & Rebekah Stringer
Alderman Smith School

Racism

Racism is cruel,
Racism is harsh,
They're all like us,
You can't tell them apart,
They are black, we are white,
What's the difference?
We are the same.

Lewis Malkin (12)
Alderman Smith School

Untitled

The beautiful white house,
Bullets all around,
Surrounded by green lawns,
Inside, none alive to be found.

The beautiful white house,
Screams come from inside,
Surrounded by green lawns,
Not many left that are alive.

Clancy Ashby, Annie Fitter & Jes Greenway
Alderman Smith School

What's It All For?

There are people in Iraq
Who are fighting the war
There are people in the world
Who don't obey the law

Why can't we end the fighting?
Why can't we end the war?
Why can't we sign a treaty?
What's all this fighting for?

Joseph Fletcher-Ward (14)
Alderman Smith School

Carbon Footprint

Carbon dioxide filling the air,
Most of us are too busy to care.
The world is becoming a much worse place,
When a disaster strikes, it'll be a slap in the face!
Energy bills soaring every day,
So many people struggling to pay.
It won't be long till the world meets its terrible fate,
So reduce your carbon footprint, before it's too late!

Sophie Reckless (14)
Alderman Smith School

War

Into war the fighting men went
From the people of the world, they were sent
Risking their lives for all their loved ones
Explosions and guns and also big bombs

Men dying and lying around
The grimness of death went silent with sound
The loss of people brings the army down in size
Injuries everywhere and the noise of cries.

Reanne Kavanagh Rowe (12)
Alderman Smith School

Auschwitz Hell!

Burning bodies all around,
Three act plays and making bands,
People screaming, a terrible sound,
Killing people with their hands.

Watching the white house fill with blood,
Dancing, singing in the sun,
Walking through the treacherous mud,
Having a laugh and lots of fun.

Demi Miller, Sian Finlayson & Jessica Eales (13)
Alderman Smith School

Planet Earth

Flowers growing, icebergs melting,
Life in the trees, is so green,
Without us knowing, nature is growing,
But soon it will be going,
Fishes swimming, penguins flapping,
Life in the cold is a breeze,
You must be kind to all living things,
That means no clutter, rubbish or anything.

Rebecca Cryer (11)
Alderman Smith School

Go Green And Go Clean

Look after our Earth,
So the children of the future will see,
A hedgerow, a panther,
A whale, a cheetah,
A beautiful clean, blue sea,
Green fields and meadows,
Clear blue skies and poppies,
Free of pollution and debris.

Leigh-Anne Cart (11)
Alderman Smith School

Green, Green, Go!

Keep our planet clean,
We like it to be green,
We need to recycle,
So it can be a better place,
Environment is important,
We need the place to be friendly,
We need it to be a better world,
To keep the grass green and clean.

Daniel Gandy (11)
Alderman Smith School

Recycle

R ecycle, recycle
E veryone recycle, it's good for the environment
C lear your house of jars and paper and cardboard
Y ou recycle and live more
C ans, cardboard are all good things, so
L et's recycle and help the
E nvironment, yeah!

Callum Treadwell (11)
Alderman Smith School

A Green Recycle

Think - stop littering!
Pollution is getting worse
Animals are becoming extinct
Because of pollution
People homeless
Make our environment friendlier
Stop CO_2!

Bethany Patrick (11)
Alderman Smith School

Recycling

Recycle, recycle,
It's good to recycle,
Recycling makes the world a better place,
It makes the world go round.

If you recycle,
You'll get the people out of poverty,
You shall see,
They shall be having a cup of tea.

You'll make the dumps get smaller,
And the homeless,
Shall have a home again.

Please recycle,
The plastic, the glass,
The clothes and the paper.

Recycle!

R ecycling makes the world go round
E nvironmentally friendly
C lothes can be recycled
Y ou can get the people out of poverty
C limate change can be stopped
L itter is a horrible waste
E xtinction to animals can be worked on.

Anisah Shehzad (11)
Alexandra High School

Homeless Feel The Pain

Homeless people in
Search of food
Crying and helpless
In such a low mood

Homeless people
Nowhere to go
Searching for a place
They can call home

Homeless people
No family, no friends
Wishing they could turn back
To make amends

Homeless people
Sleeping rough
Park benches
Cardboard boxes
They're not fussed

Homeless people
Out in the rain
Wishing people
Could feel their pain
Wanting a home again!

Homeless people
Finding the light
They can see happiness
In sight
With help from other people
The future is bright!

Jeevan Athwal (11)
Alexandra High School

Animals And Extinction

All animals can be cute,
But some people don't think they are,
So they treat them badly,
To help the animals in the world,
All you have to do
Is make sure you clean up all your litter,
So animals don't get injured,
Let animals live how they want to live,
Otherwise you will kill them all off.

And, you know if you accidentally
Drop beer nets on the floor
And can't be bothered to pick them up
You can cause a bird to become trapped
Because the circle can easily
Go around a bird's neck.

The big question is . . .
Are you doing enough to help animals?
If not - then start!
You could be saving animals
From *extinction!*

Georgie Withers (12)
Alexandra High School

Recycle

All you have to do is:
Reduce, reuse, recycle.

Reduce is the one
Where you reduce the amount
Like dustbins and all types of landscapes.

Reusing is where you use it twice
And not recycle the first time
If you can use it again.

Recycle is when you send it away
And do your bit every day, anyway.

Chloe Williamson (11)
Alexandra High School

17

Where Have They Gone?

Where have they gone?
Where have they gone?
Where are all the animals?
Tigers, seals and eagles,
Where have they gone?
Where have they gone?
Cheetahs, bees and bears,
They're not down in their lairs,
I think they're dead,
They were underfed,
Probably killed by a harpoon,
They're all going to die too soon,
Where have they gone?
Where have they gone?
We must stop this suffocation,
We need to know more about the species information,
What will we do without them?
Our beauty, prize and gem,
Oh, where have they gone?
Oh, where have they gone?

Tanzeela Toseef (12)
Alexandra High School

Recycle!

Recycle, recycle, recycle! The benefits are secure,
Recycle, recycle, recycle! You're helping the world, for sure!

War, war, war! To show off their strength and their might,
War, war, war! It gives people such a fright!

Litter, litter, litter! The streets used to be clean,
Litter, litter, litter! Now they're uninviting and mean!

Poverty, poverty, poverty! This is horrible, but true,
Poverty, poverty, poverty! Who can help? Me and you!

Us, us, us! We all should do our bit,
Us, us, us! In keeping the world fit!

Ethan Joseph Jones (11)
Alexandra High School

What About Others?

Some people are homeless,
Out on the streets,
Scrabbling for food,
No one to turn to,
All alone and helpless.

We are so lucky,
Compared to them,
We have money - they don't,
We have food and shelter - they don't.

The government have lots of money,
Can't they provide basic flats,
From the money they have?
The homeless have nothing, no money,
For food, shelter and even clothes.

Can't the government do just one thing
And make a homeless person's dream come true -
Provide them with a lifeline.

Lauren Shaw (11)
Alexandra High School

The World Could Be A Better Place

The world could be a better place
So start by recycling your litter
Don't have racism, it only makes you bitter
Pollution doesn't make any gain
It only makes a climate change
Poverty is putting us in distress
Making most people homeless
Pollution in cars, this isn't the way
Use a bike and make it go away
Whether you're happy or sad
This poem is something that people had
So try your best and don't make us sad
Every bit helps, not matter how small
Just keep trying and we will conquer them all!

Chelsea Cook (11)
Alexandra High School

Keep The Planet Breathing

Fumes from cars and planes make you choke,
We treat our planet like it's a joke,
Plastic bags and bottles everywhere,
People discard them like they just don't care.
Holes in the ozone, the Earth's getting hot,
It's time to take care of it, it's all we've got,
Ice caps melting, seas begin to rise,
The land's disappearing before our eyes.
Species dying out, plants and crops wilt,
We can't ignore it, we all share the guilt,
So do your bit, it's easy to begin,
Put your paper, bottles, cans in the recycling bin,
Walk when you can, you don't always have to drive,
It all helps the planet to stay alive.
Never waste electricity and gas,
Recycle all your garden waste and grass,
Go outside and plant a tree,
Help keep the planet breathing, for you and me.

Joely Wade (11)
Alexandra High School

The Panda

The panda sits in her tree
With her baby she needs to be free
She chews on bamboo
While she lives in the zoo!
The people stand and watch them play
Come to visit day after day
So cuddly and cute, the children say
We hope the panda is here to stay!

The panda looks back at the crowd
And thinks that they're awfully loud
She longs for the quiet
To enjoy her bamboo diet
But the threat of *extinction*
Means she's not allowed.

Lucy Pearson (11)
Alexandra High School

20

Animals And Extinction

A nimals are coming to extinction
N aughty poachers are killing them
I n the world today there are only 3,100 rhinos left
M onkeys like the orang-utan are becoming extinct
A lso Siberian tigers are being hunted for their fur
L eopards, whales, pandas, they're all becoming extinct
S o how can you help?

E lephants are killed for their tusks
eX tra large homes of animals are being cut down
T oo much litter is being thrown into the water
I t's not fair for the animals
N ow macaws are being captured for pets
C an you help?
T hink how you would feel to be kill or captured
I believe that we can make the world a safer place for animals
O nly you have the choice to make a difference
N ever give up!

Kayleigh Hartwell (11)
Alexandra High School

Earth, All It Takes Is One . . .

E very three seconds in Africa, a child dies
A ny day now, the Amazon will disappear
R ain water will fall for 2mm a year in Africa
T ibetan monks die, trying to be freed
H undreds of children in Zimbabwe will be orphans
    Because of their president

How can this be stopped?
What will be done?
All it takes is one!
One to shout out, 'Stop!'
One to save a rainforest,
One to save the Arctic,
Earth, all it takes is one . . .

Grace Wilkinson (11)
Alexandra High School

Recycle, It's Easy!

Recycle, recycle, recycle
That's all you hear out there
Why should we all recycle?
We don't really give a care

Think about the future
The life your kids will live
To slow down global warming
What a wonderful gift to give

Five minutes daily sorting
It doesn't take a lot
To give us all a future
That isn't extra hot

So think about recycling
An easy job to do
To help out all your family
But most of all, help you.

Bethany Skelton (12)
Alexandra High School

Despair Of The Homeless Man

He's so alone,
So cold,
In utter despair,
Just lying there.

The look on his face,
Like he's never won a race,
All the non-stop gambling,
Took his life away.

Can we help him?
Help him get a job and a home,
Donate some fancy clothing
And help him start a new life.

Billy Lacey (11)
Alexandra High School

On Their Behalf

Baa! Miaow! Woof! Squeak!
They lie there, half-dead, half-beat,
Who would do such a thing?
People who are vain and should be punished!
Don't animals deserve love?
Sometimes, people sit and wonder . . .
Why? Why do it? It doesn't prove anything about yourself.
What if animals were us and we were animals
And they started to beat us?
We wouldn't like it, would we!
It just goes to show that in this world . . .
Love is true and that love is kindness
But wouldn't it be nice to have an animal to share it with?
Just live your life as you want, happy, fun, love,
Share the love you have with an animal,
A cat, dog, rabbit and in return . . .
The animal will love you . . .

Georgia Lamara Pearce (11)
Alexandra High School

Climate Change Can Make A Difference

Rain, rain, rain,
Yet more rain again,
Where is the sunshine
That I could call mine?

To make me nice and warm,
Hearing my dad mow the lawn,
Instead we have worry,
Once the ice has become slurry.

You can't tell the difference
Between autumn and spring
The birds are so confused
They don't know when to sing!

What more can we do?
Can someone please give us a clue?

Laura-Jayne Cowley (11)
Alexandra High School

23

Save The Animals

Save the animals,
They are becoming extinct,
You wouldn't like it,
So you must think,
Think of the future
And what it holds,
As there will be no more animals left,
Young or old,
Save our animals,
They are becoming extinct,
Save the future,
What they live in,
Save all our land
And ice caps alike,
Save it for our future,
For that is life.

Tanya Martin (11)
Alexandra High School

Tomorrow

As mankind does another tribal dance
In hope of something turning in the weather,
I wonder if the Earth still has a chance?
Its people cannot seem to work together,
It seems the voice of reason is too meek
And never heard above the cry for money,
A prophet needs to stand up tall and speak,
Destroy the myth of ageless milk and honey.
The lessons learned are falling with the trees
And swept out with sawdust we should cherish,
No thought of what we pour into the seas,
Or how a future world will starve and perish.
I wish some companies would see the sky,
The colour blue, to symbol earthly sorrow,
But wanted to be happy, not to die,
The answer will be written, tomorrow.

Billy Cope (12)
Alexandra High School

No More Pollution

N is for no more pollution
O is for ozone

M is for more walking
O is for on your legs, not the car
R is for replace the car for your legs
E is for environment

P is for pollution
O is for original ways
L is for love the environment you're in
L is for live in a clean environment
U is for universe
T is for totally clean
I is for invisible rubbish
O is for on your bike more
N is for nature.

Jessica Paige Whitehouse (11)
Alexandra High School

Rubbish!

Cigarettes out of windows,
Chewing gum on floors,
Cans in the gutter,
Old wooden doors,

Banana skins on pavements,
Bottles on the street,
Crisp packets blown in bushes,
Chip papers at my feet,

Litter in my garden,
Don't throw it away, that's the key,
Make our world a tidier place,
It's all rubbish to me!

Sophia Benbow (11)
Alexandra High School

Recycling Litter

Please recycle,
It's good for the environment,
Please recycle,
It's good for the environment.

Litter is bad,
It's not good,
Please recycle
And you'll be good.

Recycle, recycle,
Please recycle today,
I hope you recycle,
Please recycle today!

Mark Jones (11)
Alexandra High School

Our Environment

E nd of war
N o one is doing enough
V ery bad things will happen if we don't stop it
I sense it's time we should do something
R ainforests must be saved
O nly humans can stop it
N eed you to help
M oney is needed to go to charity
E xtinction of animals must be stopped
N ot enough is being done
T rash must be put in the bin.

Tom Fleetwood (11)
Alexandra High School

Our Environment

E xplore
N ever drop litter
V ery precious
I nteresting
R espect
O nly one
N ever give up helping
M oonlight
E njoy
N ot to ruin
T ake care.

Emma Garrett (11)
Alexandra High School

Help!

Help! I'm dying, save me,
My creatures, my people too,
We are all dying, because of most of you!
Stink! The pollution chokes me!
It makes me feel very ill,
My ozone layer thins
And stops protecting all of you!
All my pets around the world
Are dying 'cause of your rubbish!
Help me save them before it's too late,
If you don't, you're making a big *mistake!*

Natalie Ellis (11)
Alexandra High School

Environment

E veryone seems to be alright
N ot for some people, where the future's not so bright
V arieties of people live with a disease
I n the forest people cut down trees
R eal people are always starving
O r population in poor countries are halving
N ot many people recycle which is bad
M any people think that is very sad
E very single person has a voice
N ow speak up and make the right choice
T ry and find it in your heart to save this planet!

Kyle Harris (11)
Alexandra High School

Why?

In the huge world, no one seems to care,
The natural parts of this Earth; the rainforests, the seas, the air,
All are being destroyed!
The rainforests are being wrecked, just to get paper,
Why don't people understand the word . . . *recycle?*
Climate change, climate change,
Well, what can I say?
There's big gas-guzzlers zooming really fast,
Wider than the road,
Why do people need them?
Nobody knows!

Esme Hill (11)
Alexandra High School

Help Them!

Think of all the animals in this world,
No home, no love, think how *you* would feel if that were you,
Most animals are on the edge of extinction because of their fur,
Doesn't anyone care?
Fish, birds and even cats and dogs,
Get caught in the plastic beer holders,
The least you can do is cut them up!
Lots of animals are on the streets scavenging
For food and water, they drink from puddles,
Animals are for life, not just for Christmas,
Help them!

Katie Dunn (11)
Alexandra High School

The Homeless

Lonely in the night
Stars are shining bright
People down below
Searching for a home
No one will let them in.

No shoes, no socks, no clothing
Outside in the rain, they're soaking
They starve all through the week
They're lucky to find something to eat.

These people need your help!

Abigail Brookes (11)
Alexandra High School

Stop The War

S oldiers fighting
T errorists plotting
O ut of control
P oliticians deciding

T error on innocent faces
H atred everywhere
E vil things happening

W hy do we fight?
A rmies struggling
R ight or wrong?

Jack Fox (11)
Alexandra High School

Homeless

By yourself at a dark street light,
Hoping you'll find help that night,
Wanting someone there by you.

Wishing your dream will come true,
All your things have gone to rot,
No food, no drink,
No help at all,
Life is hard.

So take my hand,
You've got help, my dear.

Lauren Marie Scott (11)
Alexandra High School

Help The Animals

If you want to help animals,
Give this a try,
Adopt one of them,
Don't let them die,
If you don't adopt an animal,
They could become extinct
And if that happens,
The world will have lost a species
In a blink!
So, adopt an animal!

Lucy Edwards (11)
Alexandra High School

Recycle

R ecycle to help save the world
E veryone recycling and working together will make a better environment
C an we all take part by doing our jobs by recycling
Y ou can do something to help, even if it's only a little job so put in the effort
C ome on, we can all do it, have faith
L et's get together and all recycle
E veryone can do it!

Danny Joe Griffiths (11)
Alexandra High School

Our Environment

Our environment needs some TLC,
So pick up all the litter you see,
Make this place nice and clean,
Don't even think about being cruel or mean!
Think how the climate could change,
The weather will end up being really strange!

Eve Allsop-Buckler (11)
Alexandra High School

The World

Think of the world without pollution,
That would be the solution,
To all the world's problems and needs,
You say you don't believe it,
But really you just can't face it,
We can cut down on industrial waste,
Use cars less and walk a bit more,
It would work if we all gave it a try,
So, come on, help! Just don't be shy!

Hayley Bradnick (11)
Alexandra High School

Disasters Are Everywhere

The Earth is dying, someone help!
Pollution is growing, what shall we do?
Everything is dying,
From sunlight to soil,
Bit by bit flakes off
From objects floating in the air,
Lord, help us, hear our prayer,
Save the world from dying from despair,
For disasters are everywhere.

Siobhan Welborn (12)
Alexandra High School

Racism

Being racist is a crime,
We do it all the time,
Black or white,
We always fight,
But that does not
Make things right.

Bethany Gilby (11)
Alexandra High School

Like Anger

It's horrible; all you cause is lost people everywhere
The people are angry and tearing out their hair
The children need care
I bet they think it's not fair
The people's clothes smell
They need water, but the only water supply
Is from the well
Their lives must be Hell!

Craig Barnes (11)
Alexandra High School

The Monkeys

A rainforest tree goes down,
The monkeys frown,
You've just chopped down their food and home,
Now with no home, they stand alone,
They'll have to start again,
Wasting time, searching for a new den,
This cycle keeps going on and on,
Before we know it, *all* the trees will be gone!

James Moore (12)
Alexandra High School

Stop Extinction

We think rainforests are just wood for fires,
Or houses for small empires,
But inside that forest, where the houses were made,
Animals are being woken,
To see their houses being broken,
We do not care about other species on the Earth,
That's why we are killing nature's birth,
We need to stop, today and tonight,
So not all animals fall out of sight!

Joe Haycock (11)
Community College Bishop's Castle

Day After Day!

You cut it all down,
Day after day,
Day after day,
You take it away.

You're making them pay,
Day after day,
Day after day,
You take them away.

The oil floods in,
Day after day,
Day after day,
You put things in the bin.

We should stop all this now,
I can't take much more,
Blood is spread,
Day after day,
Day after day,
You make me pay.

Isobel Brick (11)
Community College Bishop's Castle

Two Lives

I see trees of green,
You see trees of black,
I see red roses
And I see roses of black and grey.

I'm seeing cars,
You're seeing tanks,
I see a cloud of white
And you see a cloud of black.

I think to myself,
That my life is wonderful
And then I think,
Are you dead?

Craig Harris (12)
Community College Bishop's Castle

Nature

You give us air,
You give this world
We should now be better
To appreciate it all.

You give us water
You give us food
Now we should know
What to do.

You give us animals
You give us fruit
We should care for the animals
And all the fruits.

Thank you for the world
Thank you for the day
Thank you for the night
When we sleep without a fright.

Tiraj Swali (12)
Community College Bishop's Castle

Murder

English soldiers fighting,
Fighting for their life,
Worrying about their family,
'How is my wife?
Does she miss me?
As I miss her?'
Writing letters every night,
The sound of gunfire,
A distant echo in time,
'I miss you my love,
I hope to come home soon.'
This war is awful
This is not about peace, nor war,
We fight but don't unite,
This is murder.

Polly Godfrey (13)
Community College Bishop's Castle

I Live In Poverty

I lay here, still as concrete
As every bone stiffens
I look up at the sky
As I cry
I wished for a
Bed
But never to come
I wished for
A blanket
But never to come
I wished for
A home
But never to come
I wish for a family
But never ever to come
You are the lucky ones
While I live in poverty.

Holly Ewers (12)
Community College Bishop's Castle

War

Gunshots,
Lives lost,
Trees burning
Mud churning
Corpse filled ground
Earth shattering sound
Explosions of fire
The corpse hill getting higher
Splashes of red
So many dead
On the black floor
War!

Lydia Rogers (12)
Community College Bishop's Castle

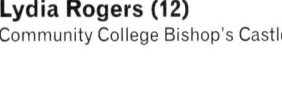

War Galore

We fight, with all our might,
We throw, we explode,
We kill, blood we spill,
Explosions galore,
Is this the beauty of war?

Grenades will fly, people will die,
Blood in the streets, where people did lie,
Bullets in chests, legs, arms and thighs,
Guns will fire, going higher and higher,
Huge piles of blood and gore,
Is this the beauty of war?

Sean Livingstone (12)
Community College Bishop's Castle

In Poverty

I have no home
I have no future
I have nothing

I am small
I am helpless
I am ill

I don't have a family
I don't have medicine
I don't have a TV

I live in poverty!

Abi Bramah-Taylor (12)
Community College Bishop's Castle

37

No Wildlife

I'm sitting outside my house
With the wildlife all around,
Rabbits, birds, squirrels and pheasants,
One year from now
I'm sitting in the same place,
But something's changed,
There's no wildlife.
No rabbits, birds, squirrels or pheasants,
No cockerels with their wild crescents,
No, nothing here at all,
No animals!

William Fairbanks (11)
Community College Bishop's Castle

Environment

E verything is getting worse
N atural resources going
V ision of the future is bad
I ce caps melting
R ubbish thrown
O zone dying
N atural Earth, going, going, gone
M ore electricity, less time
E xtinction
N ature dying
T rees cut down.

Hannah Cooke (12)
Community College Bishop's Castle

TV

Green is for going, leaving me running,
Red is for stop leaving me on standby,
No colour is for off, sleeping and saving my energy.

Harry Curtis-Evans (11)
Community College Bishop's Castle

Cardboard Box Street

As we walk to the big city,
We think it's all glam and showbiz,
But as we walk through a street,
I just see boxes,
With people in them,
Begging for money,
A man comes up to me,
I give him a tenner,
He hugs me,
He smells of beer and sadness,
Why can't everyone just give money to the cardboard box street?

Katherine Dawson-Clarke (12)
Community College Bishop's Castle

Save Our World

E veryone is destroying our planet
N o one should litter or pollute
V aluable time of Earth's life is being wasted
I t would help a lot if we tried a bit harder
R eally, we need to be protecting our world
O h, what a shame it would be
N ot having a planet any longer
M any people are dying because of us
E very country at war with another
N obody brave enough to help
T errible things that *we must stop!*

Amber Lloyd (12)
Community College Bishop's Castle

The Smoky Town Change

I live in a smoky town
I think it will never change
I tell them, don't use your cars, walk
But then I have a plan
My plan was sure to work
I put a lock on their cars
That was sure to work
The next morning, I could see a blue sky
All the people came out
Then I unlocked their cars
And they never used their cars again.

Tomos Evans (11)
Community College Bishop's Castle

He Gave Us

He gives us life
And we keep fit,
He gave us a world
And we're destroying it.

He gives us rainforests,
We cut down the trees,
He gives us animals
We steal the honey from the bees.

He made the past
So we'll make the future!

Kathryn Emerson (13)
Community College Bishop's Castle

War

Bang! Bang! Bang!
Go the enemy's guns
We fight back
And the enemy runs
War is destructive
Negative and bad
It doesn't do anything
But make people sad
People are dying every day
When can we have our say?

Niall Thomas (12)
Community College Bishop's Castle

The War Of 1920

I jumped down behind an old shed
I wish that I could be tucked up in bed.
It's the war of 1920
I'm here with my mates, Ed and Henry.
I peeped all the way around,
I heard a bang; Henry was down.
The war's all over,
I jumped out of cover.
What has just happened?
The world is over!

Katie Appleby (11)
Community College Bishop's Castle

The World Two

You give us life
But we commit suicide
You give us love
But we give you war
You give us plants
That we turn into drugs
You give us sky
But we give you clouds of smoke
You give us food
But we give you rubbish.

Naomi Jones (13)
Community College Bishop's Castle

The World

As we lie asleep in our beds
The world is crashing down around our heads
The lights are on
The icebergs will soon be gone
The world is dying
But are we trying
To stop this problem spreading
For the task of saving the world
There is no queue
Cos the person for the job is . . . *you!*

Gemma Murphy (11)
Community College Bishop's Castle

The Recycle Poem

I give you pigs, cows and lambs
Only for good use,
You give me sausages, beef and mince back.

I give you mountains,
You give me quarries.

I give you trees,
You give me paper,
But you can recycle it,
It's never too late!

Jay Lane (11)
Community College Bishop's Castle

Paper

I'm a piece of paper
I get used twice
I got recycled
Better for everyone

I came back again

Someone used one side of me
And threw me away
Then I get thrown in a landfill
Till I rot away.

Leanne Green (12)
Community College Bishop's Castle

Pollution

P oisonous air
O ut of control
L ittering
L ess caring
U nhealthy
T otally hazardous
I can't breathe
O ff the scale, terrible and dangerous
N egative in every way!

Ed Marston (11)
Community College Bishop's Castle

Recycle Fast

R ecycling; not everyone does it
E veryone needs to do their bit
C limate change is coming fast
Y ou and me need to last
C ans and cardboard we can recycle these
L et us have a good future, please
I ce is melting as we speak
N o one wants the sea to leak
G o and get your cans right now and put them in the green bin now!

Lydia Morray (11)
Community College Bishop's Castle

Litterbugs

L itter kills animals, even the smallest size
I think litter's bad, we need to get it right
T ime is ticking, litter doesn't say any lies
T ime to think about those big holes in the ground
E at what you want, but don't throw it around
R emember to do your bit
   Otherwise the world will have a fit!

Chloe Peers (11)
Community College Bishop's Castle

Recycling

R ecycling is great
E veryone should recycle
C an recycling help the world
Y es, I think it can
C an people stop digging holes in the ground
L uckily, they can
I wish they could stop polluting the planet and recycle
N ow if everyone helps the planet will not be polluted
G o and fight for our planet!

Kirsty Broomfield (11)
Community College Bishop's Castle

Pollution

We give rubbish
The world gives us air
But we don't care.

Ice melting
Animals dying
People homeless.

We give litter and pollution
Pollution - stop, just stop!

Anna Ziko (11)
Community College Bishop's Castle

Picture

The world is like a beautiful picture,
But the picture is fading and rotting,
Disintegrating into a dark hole
And we are the ones crumpling up the picture,
We are the ones letting it disintegrate into a hole
We are . . .
Help us!

Charlotte Kennedy (11)
Community College Bishop's Castle

Pure Madness

A shout, a scream,
A camouflaged machine,
It roars and bangs,
Its metal shield clangs!

You can hear the soldiers whining,
The women and children are crying,
We can stop this terrible madness,
Let's bring peace to the world!

Tamsin Ockenden (11)
Community College Bishop's Castle

Help Us!

You killed me, you took me away, you think I'm money,
You're just encouraging people to think this is funny!
You ignored me when I let out a moan
And the reason for this is you took me from my home!
When you were done, you left me by myself and all alone,
There to rot, just skin and bone!
We must stop today and tonight,
Before us animals fall out of sight!

Bethan Gehlen (11)
Community College Bishop's Castle

Our World

Our world is green, but our thoughts are red,
Technologies zooming in the back shed,
We think about cars and stars
And in his room, my brother plays his electric guitars,
Our world is slipping in the melting ice,
On the brink of a fall, it can't be nice,
Meanwhile, in our house, the lights are on,
We're watching TV, blissfully unaware of the time ticking on!

Eleanor Carty (12)
Community College Bishop's Castle

It Used To Be

It used to be cool, now it's warm.
It used to be clean, now it's polluted.
It used to be fresh, now it's rotten.
Fish used to be in water, now they're in cans.
There used to be lush, snowy mountains, now they're hot quarries.
We should walk and use public transport.
We should put rubbish in bins,
Not rivers and streams.

Oliver Jones (11)
Community College Bishop's Castle

Extinction

I've been on this world longer than you,
But yet, I am dying out.
I tried to survive,
But when I come back from the brink,
You push me back down,
Like water in a sink!
From an animal's point of view . . .
Extinction!

Tabitha Storm (11)
Community College Bishop's Castle

War Must Stop!

You can hear the shells going off
The bullet hitting innocent people
The enemy team had captured the church steeple
So we need to work fast
If we can keep people to last
Fighting must stop
To keep everything on top!

Todd Langley Tanner (12)
Community College Bishop's Castle

Animal Cruelness

We need to stop this now
All the cruelness and the sound
We don't think do we?
As we chop the trees down
The sound of the cries
The animals creep in terror
Stop this now!

Jessica Kent-Nye (11)
Community College Bishop's Castle

Black And White

One is white
One is black
Both are equal.

White and black
Both are colours
But are still people.

Hannah Pidduck (11)
Community College Bishop's Castle

War

Bombing is about killing
It's about people dying
Every day just for us

We watch them on TV, suffering
People with broken arms and legs
People are dying every day.

Chantal Locke (12)
Community College Bishop's Castle

You Can Help!

Car emissions, game additions
You should get outside and walk
While you're walking, don't start talking
Think of how you can help!
Help the world stay around for future generations
And for your grandchildren and mine.

Chris Irving (11)
Community College Bishop's Castle

Litter

L ucozade bottles thrown on the floor
I t helps if that doesn't happen anymore
T idy it up into a recycling bin
T hen we will be
E co
R ecycling people!

Connor Jones (11)
Community College Bishop's Castle

Litterbugs

L ots of rubbish
I n the skip
T he rubbish skips to the dump
T he dump smells a bit bitter
E very day it gets bigger
R emember to recycle.

Mitchell Thomas (12)
Community College Bishop's Castle

Sparking To A Comfortable Halt

Spinning for millions
    Our brief second here
        Destruction of our past, present and future.

Spark of electricity
    Sends our world up in smoke
        So many billions before us
            They survived fine.

We are making our lives better . . .
    Maybe . . .
            But ending it short.

So spinning for millions of generations
    Yet we who make life better
        Make life worse
            Our pleasure and comfort.

Actually, the beast who grows inside us
    And steadily unsettles the comforts
        With the signs
            Passing unnoticed
                With the steady throb
                    Of every heartbeat.

Now a racing heart
    Growing steadily with more fury than the last.

Spinning for millions
    Slowing down
        With every
            Tiny
                Little
                    Man-made pleasure.

Andy Main (13)
Ellesmere College

Choices

We are on a balance
Caught between destruction and redemption
It is our choice
Between what is right and what is the cause of death
Will we make the right choice?

Stuck on a line
One deed could make the difference
Make the change
Ask the question; what is the cost?
Will it take over your life?

All it takes is awareness
Vigilance of things you can change
It isn't hard
Why should you do something different?
Why choose wrong?

Choose to turn off a light
Choose to pick up litter
Choose to change the tone
Of your family and friends
Don't destroy the planet; destroy global warming.

John Paul (13)
Ellesmere College

Do You?

Do you turn off your TV?
Do you turn off the lights?
Do you have a shower instead of a bath?
Because I do.
It is the little things that make a difference
We need to start *now!*
Do you recycle?
Do you use less paper?
Do you cut down trees?
Do you work in a factory?
Think about all these things and save the planet!

Connor Shields (11)
Ellesmere College

Ask Me How

Recycle, recycle
Ask me how
Recycle, recycle
See paper in the bin
Put it in the recycle bin
Pick it up, put it in
Pick it up, put it in the recycle bin

Be super kind
Have recycle in your mind
You don't need to be Superman
Just neighbourhood man
It's not sad, it's not uncool
It's not hard to walk to school
Walk to your local shop.

Recycle, recycle
Ask me how
It doesn't cost
Not being green is a threat to the human race
Even more than wars and aliens
So use your big green machine.

Richard Rimmer (13)
Ellesmere College

The Green Story

Green, green grass
Be green and recycle
Black, black oil, coal
Hard to be unkind
Dig for it
Ice caps melting
Flash floods
Loss of life
Shed blood
Not my family
Why yours?

Cameron Beswick (12)
Ellesmere College

Simple Things Make A Difference

The icebergs melt and the polar bears die
The trees fall down and begin to cry
The dolphins are trapped behind the nets
The whales are being killed by poachers.

The charities are there to help
So don't just watch their adverts
Do something and you will make a difference
They are not just there to decorate lamp post and TV screens.

The rats in test labs never see sunlight
The monkeys who test if helmets work
The wild elephants killed for their tusks
The baby seals killed for the 'fun' of sport.

You could donate some money
Or rescue a dog from the RSPCA
You could adopt a wild animal
Or sponsor a rare breed.

It could be as simple as switching off a light switch
Or turning off the TV at the plug.

Eleanor Biggs (14)
Ellesmere College

Stop!

It is time for us to act,
Let us all join hands and make a pact.
We need to make our country clean
And can only do this by turning green.
For our children, we must change our ways,
Or our generation will end Earth's days.

It is time for us to act
And take no industrial impact.
No terrorists to attack our living hand,
Let's give them no helping hand.
Credit crunch is eating our money,
If we don't share our future, it won't be fair.

Richard Belcher (14)
Ellesmere College

Opposites

The pain we cause to others
Stop the badness
It kills their soul
Stop the badness
The Amazon falls
Stop the badness
Antarctica melts
Stop the badness
Recycle
Start the goodness . . .

Help an orphan
Start the goodness
Save the animals
Start the goodness
Stop using all the fossil fuels
Start the goodness
People need help
We all need help
From others and ourselves.

Georgina Ottaway (13)
Ellesmere College

Save The Earth

S ave the Earth
A nd be grateful
V ery quickly are we changing
E ver will we learn from our mistakes

T he Earth is dying
H elp it now
E ver thought about recycling

E ver considered putting rubbish away
A ct now and make a difference
R emember to tell others to do the same
T he Earth needs help desperately
H elp it now and live in a better place.

Georgia Stackhouse (12)
Ellesmere College

Recycle

The Earth that once reigned victorious,
Now lies in the dustbin,
With all the other rubbish,
Unrecycled,
Why don't you stop it?
Recycle!

Blood scatters the floor,
As litter,
It has a better body,
Than the floor,
Why don't you stop it?
Recycle!

Green box; metal,
Blue box; paper
Brown box; glass
Why don't you stop it?
Recycle!

Bethany Lyttle (12)
Ellesmere College

Patching Up

Stand alone
Or stand together

Make a change
Or a difference

Wipe a tear
Or clean a flood

Feed a child
Or a nation

Put a plaster on a scar
Or patch up the shattered Earth

We can do more
Together!

Kate Parry (13)
Ellesmere College

Extinct Animals

More animals are extinct now,
Than there used to be,
No dodos on the land,
And no turtles in the sea.

Rainforests are disappearing,
Cut down by greedy men,
But when the last rainforest goes,
We'll all be sorry then!

The passenger pigeon is no longer seen,
The Barbary lion is no more,
No longer will we see it hunt,
No longer will we hear it roar.

More animals are extinct now,
Than there used to be,
What can we do to stop this?
The answer's up to you and me.

Catriona Jones (11)
Ellesmere College

Don't Drop Litter

Don't drop litter, it's not good
You should do what you should
Put it in the bin
Release your sin
Because little birds die in a plastic bottle
Put it in the bin, just give it a throttle
Don't drop litter, it's not good
You should do what you should
Put it in the bin
Release your sin
Because animals nest in a crisp packet
Then they die and that is it
Because they harshly suffocate
So why don't you shut the gate on . . .
Litter!

Tom Willett (11)
Ellesmere College

The Green Poem

For the last few years I've been trying
Trying to stop the rubbish, the waste, but they didn't listen
And now they regret dropping that litter or driving to that place.

Now they listen when there's nothing much they can do
'The damage has been done,' I said
You didn't listen
You shouted at me and sent me away
And said that's all you wanted to hear.

And now you have to hear what I have to say
Why not before? Why now? Why now? There's no way
I tried to explain if you did that you would regret it
But you did it anyway.

You have ruined our Earth
Curse you . . .
I tried, I tried, I tried . . .
Why? Why? Why . . . ?

Melissa Andrews (12)
Ellesmere College

The Green Poem

If everyone recycled their glass and plastic
That would be fantastic.
Try to save your paper and card, so please do it -
It isn't very hard.
Don't throw away every day
Recycle for the nation today.
I have told you once, I have told you twice
Now I have to stop being nice.
We have too much vapour
So that is why we recycle paper.
If you see a scrap piece of waste
Don't just leave it there to turn into paste.
So, to save the world, just help me
But if you don't, I will plead and plead
Until you help me.

Jonathan Cooksey (12)
Ellesmere College

Nature's Poem

Reduce, reuse and recycle.

Reuse your paper,
Reuse your bags,
Reuse your plastic
And that would be fab.

Save the trees,
Save the plants,
Save the animals
And the land.

Keep your litter to yourself,
We want the animals to have good health.

Recycle paper,
Recycle card,
Recycle plastic
To save the world.

Melissa Burrows (11)
Ellesmere College

The End Of All

People, it is happening, the end of all,
But if we work together, we'll never fall.

How this happened, we'll always know,
But why it happened, they'll never show.

The only way to save our planet is cooperation,
Let us not fall to one greedy nation.

On our current path, the future is dark and full of wrath,
But if we change our ways,
A bright and beautiful future will shine through the haze.

People, if we don't save the world,
Our own personal Hell will unfold.

People, the end is nigh,
But if these are our last moments, then let us not lie.

Matthew Fraser-Smith (13)
Ellesmere College

58

Get The Picture

Cities
Are popping
Up. Trees are going
Down, all while we are
Sitting around. Bees are
Off, don't
Know where and
To be honest, some
Just don't care. It's kind
Of sad that all the monkeys
Are going mad. You know it's kinda
Strange, but also true, all these things
Are
Down
To
You!

Kieran Smith (12)
Ellesmere College

Ticking Time Bomb World

Polluting towers infinitely high
Whole forests are uprooted
Fire and burning gas is raging
And we praise it
We plundered and pillaged
Our greatest treasures and gifts
Who knows how long we can exist
In our own ticking time bomb world
With a little more care and guidance
From adults and God up above
We can pull down the towers and factories
And watch the trees grow tall again
With wind and with water
With hot ground and sun
Only we can find a way.

Lewis Allsop (13)
Ellesmere College

Stop!

People try but never succeed
To stop the destruction, havoc and war
Which some people plead
In this world we live
There is no right or wrong
To destroy homes, relationships so strong
To fix the problems we have made
Recycle, recycle, every day
Turn off taps and lights
This will help
We'd better watch out . . .
Our planet's starting to melt
Stop this destruction!
No one else can save us!

Sam Dapling (13)
Ellesmere College

My Green Machine Poem

Do you know what we are doing to the Earth?
No?
We're killing it!

Do you know what's happened to the ice?
Soon, there will only be a slice.

Do you know what's happened to the rainforests?
McDonald's cut it down for their cattle to graze.

Do you know that I recycle and ride my bicycle to work?

You can car share to share petrol.

You can do something to help all of these things.

Robbie Clarke (12)
Ellesmere College

The World Today

Come on people, we need to make our mark
Otherwise we'll have to repeat Noah's Ark
Just because of dust
The world will adjust
We all know it's a maze
Who will see us through the haze?
I'm not going to lie
But the world will die
Turn off the plugs for now
Or the world will die we all know how
So let us keep going
Or the risk of dying will keep growing.

Stuart McIlraith (13)
Ellesmere College

Global Warming

Global warming isn't hard to explain,
It leaves Mother Earth screaming in terrible dismay,
This hurts our planet in every single way,
The changes could leave us all in excruciating pain.
We need to stop now so the temperature doesn't rise,
People, plants and animals would be in terrible disgrace,
Changes in temperature due to the decreasing ozone layer,
We really don't need it to show that you care.
Mother Nature can't do it all, so let's get up and help,
We all need to try and do what is best.
Our planet Earth is precious and can't be replaced,
We need to act now, or our home will be lost in space.

Hannah Clarke (13)
Ellesmere College

Is There Hope?

As I sit looking out of the window,
I think about how lucky we are,
Thinking that it could all be gone,
Lost to mankind.
Selfishness and greed have taken over,
People are not thinking straight
And soon it could kill us all.
We are the only ones that can help,
The world disappears before our eyes,
But nobody sees.
Ask yourself, are you helping,
Or are you making things worse?

Lauren Gough (14)
Ellesmere College

All Around The World

Clean running water means happy faces
Bombing means less people in the world
Education means bright children
Murder means a guilty conscience
Clean, warm clothes means confident people
Pollution means less animals
Food and drink means a healthy body
Littering means a selfish mind
Recycling means a better world for everyone
So *think* about the world and how it is affecting you!

Eve Marley (13)
Ellesmere College

Silence

I had four beefburgers today
I drove around Britain for eight hours
I looked at a book and threw it away
I had the heating on full
I watched ten TV shows
I helped make a nuclear bomb
They let me explode it
I went home and fell asleep into nothing
From Earth
Our solar system was put into silence.

Dominic Ryder (13)
Ellesmere College

Two Hands

The bombs are falling,
The children cry,
Unaware that they have done nothing wrong.
Crash!
The beast falls to the bare ground,
Greed and fortune spread across his face.
The heat flares up, they begin to run,
But where do they go?
Two hands shake
Peace spreads across the world.

Sarah Carr (13)
Ellesmere College

Evolutionary Dead End

Algae, bacteria, invertebrates,
Fish, amphibians, reptiles,
Mammals, primates, apes, humans,
Death.

Only we can change this,
Only we can save our tiny ball of rock,
Floating through the vast expanse of space
And all life on it.

Because only we can destroy it.

Joseph Haigh (14)
Ellesmere College

The Recycling

Recycling means to use things,
Over and over again
And when I say recycle,
I don't mean your bike,
I mean the paper.

Trees are dying,
We are living.
Make the world a better place,
Recycle, recycle, recycle *now!*

Harry Whitehouse (12)
Ellesmere College

Wrecking Earth

I was walking down the street one day,
I saw a man and just had to say,
'There is a bin over there, so use it, say use it!
Polar bears are dying, glaciers are melting and sea levels rising,
So use that bin over there, say use it!'
I went to my boss one day, I stood up to him and had to say,
'Switch three of these lights off, you only need one for one room,
Penguins and seals are dying because of fumes
And the Eskimos have no homes!'

David Powell (11)
Ellesmere College

Tears

Save
Them
Stop the
Earth shedding
Tears. Light the
World. Restart the
People's lives. Open
Your heart. Stop the
Self-destruction!

Mark McBrien (13)
Ellesmere College

Green Poem

Come on boys and girls, turn off the telly
Come on boys and girls, let's work that belly
Come on mums and dads, get out of the car
Come on mums and dads, get your walking meter on far
So, come on guys, let's get fit and most of all
Let's save our planet!

George McCormack (11)
Ellesmere College

Eco Poem

Pollution is burning up the planet
This can't go on, can it?
Try to walk instead of a drive
Help to keep our planet alive

Ways to save
You must be brave
Yes, electricity will cost you less
And the planet will be the very best.

Zack Greenaway (11)
Ellesmere College

The World Today

It is time for us to act
Against the industrial fact.
Come on people, let's make a start
Or we and the Earth will shortly part.
It's time to join our hands and promise
That we, Earth's people, will help with this.
And now we need to stop world wars
And help people in a bad cause.

Berwyn Hughes (13)
Ellesmere College

Home

Forests are down
Cruelty is up
Our world is dying
While you are alive
You can help
It's your world
It's our world
It's home!

Katie Smith (14)
Ellesmere College

Recycling Rap

If you think you can get cash from trash,
Instead of it being turned into ash
You can get money from plastic
That's why I think it's fantastic
Why do people think recycling is junk?
Those people just act like punks!

Domeneco Derosa (12)
Ellesmere College

Earth Poem

Think of a time,
Many years ago,
The autumns were colder
And there was more snow.

Over the years,
The gases struck,
Through burning our rubbish,
From the garbage trucks.

Factory fumes
And aeroplanes,
Cholesterol,
In our planet's veins.

Now there's summer floods
And there's winter sun,
Is this the price we pay
For our carbon tonnes?

And what can we do?
I hear you say,
Before a higher price,
We have to pay?

Recycle waste,
Stop cutting trees,
Or the end of our Earth,
Is what we foresee.

Harriet Lahiff (14)
Evesham High School

How Long

How long will it take us,
To notice how the world is just a tiny grain of sand?
Lying abandoned on the beach, silently weeping
For protection from the sun,
Is the planet that gives us land.

How long will it take us,
To notice how the world is just a marble in a game?
Lying in wait on the sidelines, secretly weeping,
'When will they stop playing the destruction game with me?'
The others are still whole, but the Earth's not the same.

How long will it take us,
To notice how the world is just a diamond in a shop?
But the glass can only protect our world for so long
And it weeps to be sold into safer hands than ours,
We're losing it and cannot stop.

How long will it take us,
To notice how the world is just some ice cream on a cone?
It's difficult to stop from melting,
Weeping for a new ozone,
Another tricky stepping stone.

How long will it take us,
To notice how the world is just a gathering of flowers?
Sitting in silence while we destroy it,
Weeping for us to stop,
While inside polluting homes, we while away the hours.

How long will it take us,
To notice how the world is just a lion's den?
Covered in the meat, bones and blood that we have shed,
Weeping for the maid to come,
While it carries the blood of thousands, hundreds, tens.

The Earth is . . .
A tiny grain of sand,
A marble in a game,
A diamond in a shop,

Some ice cream on a cone,
A gathering of flowers,
A silent lion's den,
Weeping for . . .

Shade,
Relief,
Protection from us,
Protection from the sun,
Destruction to stop,
A cleaner planet
And it's up to us to give the world what it needs!

Orianna Walsh (13)
Evesham High School

What About The Earth?

Beyond our windows
The Earth is worried now
Our world is changing

Oceans are rising
There is too much pollution
Lands flooding slowly

Winds blowing very hard
Animals losing their homes
Trees being cut down

Let's help our world
Our planet is dying
Let's let it survive

Look after our world
Let's give it the love it deserves
Stop the pollution

Just give it respect
All it takes is love and care
So save our world

Just you on your own
One person makes a difference
Just make a difference

Let's stand by its side
And listen out for its calls
Give in to its cries.

Shereen Evans (13)
Evesham High School

69

Pip

Hello, I'm Pip the carrier bag
I come from Tesco
It is pretty boring here
Righto, I'll get back to the story

I was being made at a secret location
Then darkness overflowed my eyes
I went for a nap, then an ocean of sky poured in my eyes
Then I saw this man who grabbed me

Then I was clashed against my friends
Now we're at the checkout
We were counting how many beeps in a day
Some customer picked me up, I felt all happy inside

Then she packed me up with syrup cakes and choco brownies
Mmmm . . . the smell just drifts you away
I wanted to eat it, but I was tied up
Later, I was unpacked

After being unpacked, I felt unused again
Then I got thrown out
Quite lonely here
Later, I was blown out, I saw the sky it was . . .

. . . Black? The ocean's gone
Oh, it's nightfall, I missed the best bit of the day
I'm a bag flying in the dark sky
It was lovely, I couldn't believe it

Wow . . . look at this, I'm in a tree
With a kite, 'Hello, Kite.' No answer, I'm lonely again
Poor old me, might as well go to sleep
Oh, look at that, a shooting star, cool

It's flying over me as bright as . . .
As, well, I don't know, just bright
At first, I thought it was a chicken
No, a plane, um . . . I'm a bit mad

I was blown out of that tree, gliding in the sky
Suddenly, I'm in the deep blue sea
Oh no, I've been eaten by this shark
Oh no, what have I done?

I should have been recycled,
Poor shark thought I was a white fish

I hope he's OK
Why me? Why that shark as well?
Please, just recycle me.

Alex Harvey (13)
Evesham High School

You Don't Know Anything

You call it development,
I call it destruction,
You call it fashion,
I call it barbaric.

You think it will last forever,
I know it's running out,
You can't be bothered to change,
I can't force you to, but beware!

You call it hunting,
I call it murder,
You think nature's stupid,
I know we are just waiting.

You think there is time,
I know there is little,
You think you are moving forward,
I know you are going back.

You pretend we will survive somehow,
I think you have doomed us all,
You think there is another planet like this,
I know we can't live anywhere else.

It has already started,
It's just a matter of time,
Nature's biting back,
There's no escape now.

Unless you give back what you've taken,
You will fall victim to Gaya's wrath,
She will not watch, waiting forever,
If we do not change, she will strike.

Chloe Moore (14)
Evesham High School

71

The Match

Strike, strike, strike, lit; time is ticking, the world is go!
We are in control.
We're trying to blow it out!
We're trying to blow it out!
Puff, puff, flicker, flicker; we're trying to blow it out!
Lights left on, appliances on standby, coal-fired power stations;
Flicker, flicker, flicker,
Gulping oil, devouring coal; *flicker, flicker, flicker.*

We're trying to blow it out!
We're trying to blow it out!
Pollution, choking smog, urbanization; *flicker, flicker, flicker.*

We're trying to make it burn brighter!
We're trying to make it burn brighter!
Wind farms, solar panels, hydroelectricity; *roar, roar, roar!*

We're *still* trying to blow it out!
We're *still* trying to blow it out!
Lights *still* left on, appliances *still* on standby,
Coal *still* powering power stations; *flicker, flicker, flicker,*
Still gulping oil, *still* devouring coal; *flicker, flicker, flicker.*

We're *still* trying to blow it out!
We're *still* trying to blow it out!
There is *still* pollution, we're *still* choking on smog
And we're *still* covering our green and (once) pleasant planet
In tarmac and concrete; *flicker, flicker, flicker.*

We're trying to make it burn brighter!
We're trying to make it burn brighter!
Carbon offsetting, planting more trees
But *still* not quite doing enough;
Roar, roar, flicker.

We're *still* trying to blow it out! We're *still* trying to blow it out!
Cutting down trees,
Destroying natural beauty,
Not doing enough about it;
Flicker, flicker, flicker.

We *really, really* aren't *doing* enough about it
Flicker, flicker, smoke, gone!

Reuben Grace (13)
Evesham High School

72

The World Is A . . .

The world is a snowflake,
It is starting to bake,
Its time is ticking.

The world is a gauge,
It cries out in rage,
Its time is ticking.

The world is a bowling ball,
Always spinning until it hits a wall,
Its time is ticking.

The world is a butterfly,
It is very fragile, why?
Its time is ticking.

The world is a light,
It can go out, right?
Its time is ticking.

The world is an ice cream,
Melting in the sun's gleam,
Its time is ticking.

The world is a rainforest,
Humans cut them down, honest,
Its time is ticking.

The world is a flower,
Being baked by the sun's power,
Its time is ticking.

We warned you to stop,
But did you listen, *no!*
The world's time is ticking.

Is it worth the risk?
Will you take the blame?
Its time is ticking.

Ben Owen (13)
Evesham High School

The Dying Earth

Just think about the Earth
What can you see in your mind?
Just think about the Earth
There's something you must find.

Danger, death and destruction
Is all that's going on
The Earth is crying out for help
Soon it will be gone.

You'll probably think that we've got years
Until it's completely over
And so you go out all the time
In your Earth-destroying Rover.

Every little helps
And something must be done
The Earth is losing all its battles
And you think that we have won.

Can't you see the destruction?
Can't you see the pain?
The Earth is at the peak of death
Its emotions show in the rain.

With all the things we've done and made
We think that we're supreme
We go around killing our planet
And yet never hear its screams.

Negativity all around
Evidence everywhere
Think about the dying Earth
All the pain it cannot bare.

Think about the Earth
The dying Earth . . .

Hannah Jones (13)
Evesham High School

The World Is . . .

I give you life,
You give me pain,
I give you love,
You give me hate.

I try to change things,
You are so stubborn,
I go to give, knowing
You will take.

I know you are killing me,
You can't read the signs,
I am melting like ice,
You think I'm hard as rock.

I know I will die if you go on,
You think I'm eternally here,
I need a major change to live,
You need to help me now.

I am slowly eroding,
You are growing stronger,
I can't live with pollution,
You make new machines.

I just wish you'd change,
You were the sweetest things,
I know things change,
You have changed too much.

I am so tired,
You are so violent,
I am so sore,
You have scarred me for life.

I need your help . . .

Kim Hirons (13)
Evesham High School

Another Day

Another day has come
The birds tweeting
The sun shining
Another day has just begun

Another day is awakening
The milkman whistles as he works
The postman happily delivers away
Just think it's a brilliant start
To another day

Another day is dawning
Children wake up and get ready for school
The air around us feels so cool
Another day is becoming
And we're part of it

Another day is here
But how long will it last?
Is the crisis too late to fix?
Well, we can try

Another day as
The litter gets worse,
The polar bears suffer from global warming
But still we ignore it as it's only just
Another day

Another day
But is it?
Shout out now before it's too late
Another day
And you could help change the world.

Lauren Cowley (13)
Evesham High School

The Ballad Of A Carrier Bag!

I was at Tesco
I was picked up and used
I was in their house
I got chucked in the bin, I'm not amused.

I was blown out of the bin
I flew high in the sky
I thought I would escape and win
But landed high in a willow tree.

I was there for two weeks
I got ripped by the branches
I was split in two
Finally I got knocked out by a cat
Climbing the very same branches.

The wind blew once again
I landed in a field
In the field was a horse
The horse started playing with me
I wish he would yield.

The horse started eating me
I got in his belly
Some of me got lost
But the rest landed in the farmer's welly.

I nearly killed the horse
If I hadn't come out
The next time I hope someone recycles me
When they are out and about.

Kyle Lovegrove (14)
Evesham High School

Maths Environment Poem

Pollution + carelessness + laziness = global problems
Bad gases + hazards + ignorance = endangered animals
Harm - hurt + consideration + care = saving the world!

Elly Bishop (13)
Evesham High School

Wolf Vs Humans

The wolf hunts, stalking its prey
Its paws padding the velvet grass
Its heart pounding, waiting for a sound

Wolves are like humans

Wolves are predators, eating lots of meat
You may think they take too much
They kill innocent deer including innocent babies
They destroy
The innocent

Wolves are like humans

The difference between humans and wolves?
Global warming

We pollute the Earth
We make God angry
We destroy
We kill innocent animals
We hate

Why? Why? Why?

The Earth is like a toy
To humans
For us to beat and bully

But we are making it a ticking time bomb
Which will soon blow up!

Ryan Dennick (14)
Evesham High School

Leaves

Leaves fall on the street
Mixing with the dirty trash
Children trudging through it.

Kate Jones (14)
Evesham High School

The Ballad Of The Carrier Bag

My name is Jason, the Morrisons bag
I was being used for people to shop.
I was ripped in half
Then put in the bin, right at the top.

I was blown out of the bin
I was blown to the park.
I was stood on
I had a litter tour.

I stayed there for days
I was blown around.
The wind picked me up
To the next place to go.

I landed in the river
The birds played with me
I was taken down the river
Just to end up in the sea.

I swirled in the cold water
Twisting around a dolphin's nose.
I was extremely caught
So the dolphin can no longer breathe.

If only next time people would reuse me
Even recycle me would be nice.
I won't be blown around
And then I wouldn't cause any problems.

Katie Holder (13)
Evesham High School

The Carrier Bag

My name is Kenny
I was used to carrying shopping
Home from Tesco.
I had too many tins to carry
So I started to rip
I was screwed up and put into a bin.

I landed in a tree.

I was there for three weeks
A cat climbed into the tree and clawed me
Making me tear even more
A bird finally came and carried me away.

I landed in the sea
I was carried away by the waves
Going further and further out to sea
I felt like I was melting from the blazing sun
All of a sudden, a seal was approaching
Before I knew it, I was eaten up.

I had expanded inside the seal's stomach
No food is passing through
I think the seal is dead.

In the future
I hope my owner puts me
Surely in their recycling bin.

Carl Hiatt (13)
Evesham High School

The World

Look at what we've done,
Having all our fun,
Look at what we've created,
We might as well be cremated.

How did it come to this?
It used to be quite bliss,
It's getting rather hot,
But we can't stop.

What about the stain?
Will it remain?
Where did all the peace go?
Why couldn't we say no?

When did we turn evil?
Is it even legal?
I know it's not all bad!
But it makes me sad.

What about the seas?
Why don't we please?
What about the cars?
We're hurting the stars!

But all I really want to say
Is will we last another day?

Rachael Nicklin (13)
Evesham High School

English Maths Poem

Greenhouse gases + ice caps = melting
Litter + carelessness = waste
Disregard + ignorance = meltdown
Rising tide + ice caps melting = floods
Rising temperature + dryness = starvation
Floods + terror = panic
Heat + dryness = more bush fires
Rising temperatures + no rain = drought.

Daniel Callaghan (14)
Evesham High School

Our World Is . . .

Our world is a bin
Spilling rubbish in each day
Our world is like a big puff of smoke
Destroying our atmosphere.

Our world is like a death zone
Killing everything in its path
Our world is like a time bomb
Ready to blow any second now.

Our world is a fireball
Ready to explode
Our world is a great big world
Melting away bit by bit each day.

The world is like Hell
Burning the fossil fuels away
The world is like an egg
Ready to crack.

The world is like a hurricane
Twisting and turning and turning
Into nothingness
The world will be destroyed
If we don't stop this insanity!

James Gadsby (13)
Evesham High School

The World

T he world is being killed
H ow can we stop this?
E nergy is the key to stop this

W e could turn off lights
O r even turn the TV off standby
R enewable energy is also the key to stop
L and can be used for turbines
D anger, danger, we are all in danger!

Daniel Jelfs (13)
Evesham High School

The Dying Earth

Our world is like a ball of fire
Burning away each second
With smoke rising high
Killing things in the sky
We are wrecking the Earth

We replace fields with building sites
We change countrysides to roads
We change blue skies to grey skies
And we just pollute loads.

The Earth is dying in front of us
And we do nothing to help
All we do is dump stuff
Which we do nothing about.

If we don't change the way we live
The world will suffer, for evermore
If we keep on killing the Earth
The world will end up like a big war.

So now we have to stop
And think about what we do
Change the way the world runs
So you should help the world too.

Amy Baldwin (13)
Evesham High School

How To Solve The Puzzle

The world is a puzzle,
It takes time to put the pieces in order
And something that, at first, looks like it fits,
Can be replaced with another piece

We are the sulky child,
Too impatient to finish the puzzle
And our thrashing and moaning and bad behavior
Has resulted in us starting again

We are the cunning youth,
Too impatient to finish the puzzle
And our longing for completion,
Has resulted in us painting different pictures on the pieces

We are the content adult,
Too impatient to mind the children
And our frustration with no control
Has resulted in us clumsily muddling through

We are the wise elderly,
Too old to be paid attention
And our method and patience,
Will result in the final picture.

Helen Bates (14)
Evesham High School

Our World

The grass is not green
The Earth is not round
The sun is not hot
The sea is not high
The animals are not dying
Pollution is not in the air

If this were true
It would be OK
But it's not
So our Earth will rot away.

Matthew Jelfs (13)
Evesham High School

84

I Give You, You Give Me

I give you peace . . .
You give me war . . .
I give you food . . .
You give me litter . . .

I give you clean water . . .
You give me toxic waste . . .
I give you fresh air . . .
You give me pollution . . .

I give you land and water . . .
You give me drought and floods . . .
I give you homes and jobs . . .
You give me fire and smoke . . .

I give you transport and entertainment . . .
You give me bad language and broken glass . . .
I give you animals, rivers and parks . . .
You give me meat, black seas and graffiti . . .

I give you trees and plants . . .
You give me mud and empty fields . . .
I give you friends and family . . .
You give me *nothing* in return!

Chelsea Coupe (13)
Evesham High School

The Shining Sun, The Weeping Seas

The shining sun, the weeping seas
Why have we done this? It's asking us, please
The ice caps are melting, the sun is at its peak
If we keep doing this, the world will be weak
Why do we do this for the blame that we hold?
Do not say you don't know, because now you have been told
The polar bears are dying, their habitat demolished
It's not too late, the Earth can be repolished
So let's pull together, for the Earth's inhabitants
Let's pull together and stop these shenanigans.

Joe Heath (13)
Evesham High School

Environment - Haikus

Killing our nature
Cutting down every tree
There will be nothing

Flooding the rivers
All of the drains are now blocked
There will be nothing

Polluting the Earth
Poisonous gas in our Earth
There will be nothing

Litter on the ground
Even in the large ocean
There will be nothing

Caps melting slowly
The image will be ruined
There will be nothing

If we change all this
There will be hope in our world
There will be something!

Nina Wilks (13)
Evesham High School

The Earth

The Earth is a burning ball of fire
Which we give no attention.
Our time on the Earth is dire
It's starting to tire.
The Earth is on the brink of destruction
All we do is ignore
Here comes an eruption.
We chop down the trees with a saw
The world is bleeding
Trying to give its love
We are never believing
The Earth is like a dove.

Darren Wardle (13)
Evesham High School

Global Warming

Think, global warming
Spring, summer, autumn, winter
Warmer and warmer

Hole in the ozone
And the ice caps are melting
All of this from us

Animals extinct
We are chopping down the trees
Cutting down their homes

Animals do care
So think of them, not just you
They are dying too

Tidy up your trash
Thinking about tomorrow
Think about the world

The world is our home
You need to look after it
Or soon, it will go.

Shona McGoogan (13)
Evesham High School

The World Poem

I give you pure air,
You give me acid rain and smog,
I give you trees,
You give me paper,
I give you one place to live,
You hate me,
I give you nature,
You give me cars, industries and houses,
I give you tenderness,
You give me pain,
I give you a life,
You make me death.

Francesco Storniolo (13)
Evesham High School

I Give You . . . You Give Me . . .

I give you love
You give me war
I give you power
But you break the law
I give you opportunity
You give me one last chance
I give you new people
But you only take a glance
I give you clean water
You give me dirty water back
I give you fresh air
But you just make it black
I give you animals
You give me meat
I give you body parts
Including your feet
I give you freedom
You give me trapped
I give you everything possible
But you just threw it back.

Naomi Nobes (13)
Evesham High School

The Environment

E nergy wasting
N o one left in the future
V icious world
I gnorant human beings
R uining the planet
O ccurring pain
N either of us love
M other Nature
E ating away the Earth
N atural becoming fake
T ormenting trees.

Shahida Begum (13)
Evesham High School

What Have We Done To The World?

The world is a tennis ball being thrown into a fire
The world used to be a great desire
The world could be a better place
The world just needs to smack us in the face
The world could be nice and green
The world just needs a great big clean
The world is in such pain
The world still has a lot to gain
The world has got no power
The world just needs to have a shower
The world really needs a change
The world has no mean, mode, median and range
The world is drowning
The world is fed up with frowning
The world is not having any fun
The world really wants a gun
The world has been abandoned by the stars
The world has lots of scrapes and scars
The world needs us to reuse, recycle and reduce
The world needs us to produce.

Grant Smith (13)
Evesham High School

Responsibility

The world is in our hands,
We have to respect everything,
Not just those rock bands.

Make the world a happier place,
By recycling all we can,
To save the human race.

We love the Earth,
But is it too late,
We must try our hardest for all it's worth.

Natalie Davis (14)
Evesham High School

Give And Take

I give you love
You give me hate
I give you friends
You give me war

I give you clean air
You give me pollution
I give you cows
You give me burgers

I give you nature
You give me death
I give you plants
You give me weeds

I give you freedom
You give me slaves
I give you light
You give me dark

I give you everything possible
You just throw it back!

Jaspreet Bassi (13)
Evesham High School

Save Our Earth - Haikus

Litter not in bins
Lots of litter on the ground
Don't use fossil fuels

The world will explode
We will all die horribly
If you do not help

Please do not fly high
The world can't live without help
Stop being lazy.

Josh Macklin (13)
Evesham High School

The Big Green Poetry Machine

The world is in our hands,
Have you ever stopped to notice
All the pain the world is in?
Have you heard the monkey crying?
Because he's lost his home again,
From us chopping down the trees,
Mother Earth is unhappy with us,
We're making her bleed with pain.

Have you noticed the big change in weather?
One day we could have drought
And the next could be a flood,
The Earth is like this because we are harming it,
We need to change our ways,
To save the dying Earth,
We've got to reduce our carbon footprint
And stop litter in the street,
Today you could make a difference
And you should, maybe today or tomorrow,
But please, notice what we are doing.

Samantha Cooper (13)
Evesham High School

The Earth

The Earth is like a bowling ball,
We keep banging and bashing it,
Why do we destroy it?
We need to help it.

Pollution is like fire,
Spreading all around.
When you're in the car,
Think how you're ruining the air.

Litter is all around,
Flying on the streets.
When you see it, pick it up,
To make the Earth a cleaner place.

Kayleigh Hawkins (13)
Evesham High School

91

Save The World

Pollution is bad
It makes the world cry
Pollution is sad
But you don't know why.

You go ahead killing the Earth
We try to fix it with all our money's worth
You don't care
And it's not fair.

It's our world too
So why don't you
Stop scaring
And start sharing.

The world is great
But it does bring fate
We love it so
And we want you to know . . .

Save the world!

Denise Cowling (13)
Evesham High School

Protect Our Home

The world is ours to protect
We must keep it like our own
We are destroying the Earth this second
What are we worth
Compared with the Earth?
We need to become more eco-friendly!

We need to clear up litter
We need to ride bikes or walk
Not ride in cars and planes
We need to plant trees and flowers
Not rip them out of our peaceful ground
So, please stop and think
About our home, our wonderful world!

Matthew Carcary (13)
Evesham High School

We've Got The Whole World In Our Hands

We've turned pure rain to acid rain,
Blue skies are covered in black polluted clouds.
Green fields have turned into concrete covered towns,
Clean flowing seas have been filled with oil.

We've taken the rainforests,
Making monkeys cry out for help.
We're melting the ice caps,
Making polar bears fume with rage,
But we just ignore it for another day.

Well the day is now
And we must make a stand.
This great world we call home,
Is crumbling in our hands.

Now it's our turn,
Mother Earth gave us life.
So let's return the favour,
We've got the whole world in our hands.

Harriet Jordan (13)
Evesham High School

You Give Me

I give you freedom,
You give me war.
I give you trees,
You cut them down.
I give you food,
You give me waste.
I give you fresh air,
You give me pollution.
I give you medicines,
You give me disease.
I give you life,
You give me death.
I give you trust,
You give me lies.

Tommy Collins (13)
Evesham High School

Nature Will Hate Ya!

After ten million years, the end is nigh
If we don't act now, we will surely die
Cutting down trees will destroy what we know
Those cute polar bears will lose all their snow
Dumping muck in rivers will destroy all life
We can cut through nature just like a knife
Slaying monkeys and fish just cos we can
And so it means we are more mouse than man
So, spare a thought for old Mother Nature
If we destroy more life, she will hate ya!
If we use too much oil
The Earth will boil
Consumed with pain
Life down a drain
All animals dead
Enough said!
So, spare a thought for old Mother Nature
If we destroy more life, she will hate ya!

Stephen Bond (13)
Evesham High School

Enviro-Poem

Look at the Earth in flames,
Why are you playing sick games?
The greenhouse gases are flying up the shoot
Because you kicked them with your boot.
The Earth is getting hotter
Save us Harry Potter!

Why do you throw litter?
Why are you so bitter?
Look what you are doing
While you're sat there chewing
Save us, environmentally friendly man
Please pick up that can
Save, save, save the world
Save, save, save, save, save the world!

Hayden Causier (13)
Evesham High School

94

What Have We Done?

What have we done?
Our world is polluted
Because of all of us
We waste energy, we waste heat.

Look what we have done
The ice caps are melting
Bits falling off every day
The Earth is getting warmer and warmer.

The Earth is heating up
We are beating it up
God put us on this Earth for one thing
To look after it.

Look what we have done
We have destroyed God's Earth
The air is polluted
Our world is deleted.

Sade Gerald (13)
Evesham High School

I Give You . . . You Give Me . . .

I give you clean air
You give me pollution
I give you food
You give me waste

I give you good
You give me bad
I give you happy
You give me sad
I give you animals
You give me meat

I give you love
You give me war
I give you everything
You give me nothing more.

Hannah Kedward (13)
Evesham High School

Returning

I give you light,
You give me dark,
I give you sugar,
You give me cocaine.

I give you water,
You give me fire,
I give you warmth,
You give me cold.

I give you grass,
You give me mud,
I give you trees,
You give me paper.

I give you happy times,
You give me sad times,
I give you money,
You give me nothing.

Joe Câfearo (13)
Evesham High School

Wasted Planet

The Earth talking for itself . . .

What are you doing?
You are destroying my face?
Please stop doing that.

Precious Earth

This Earth is precious,
So why are we destroying,
This place known as home?

Wasted planet

What used to be green,
Is now the treacherous waste,
Of our home planet.

Eric Griffith (14)
Evesham High School

Every

Every snowflake is unique
The world is like no other
Every raindrop is different
The world is like no other

Every person is distinct
The world is like no other
Every butterfly is discrete
The world is like no other

Every grain of sand is singular
The world is like no other
Every leaf has different patterns
The world is like no other

The world is like no other
Why do we treat it like it is so ordinary?
The world is like no other
Everyone can help.

Amy Jones (13)
Evesham High School

Save Our Earth

Our Earth was big, round and green,
But only two of these remain.
Our Earth is burning brightly,
But it's killing our Earth almighty.
Global warming will soon take over,
Unless you don't use things, like the hoover.
We have to change our evil ways,
Or there will be polluted bays.
We have to really try to recycle,
Or you could even ride a bicycle.
Please don't kill our beautiful place,
Please try to save our human race.
So please, do something for pollution,
We have already found the solution!

Josh Higham (13)
Evesham High School

Mother Earth

What about trees?
Why are they gone?
What about our seas?
Why are they all littered?

The world is in our hands
But it's as hot as the sun.
Burning and dying all day long
The polar caps are melting, disappearing forever.

What about Mother Earth?
Why is she crying?
What about Mother Earth?
And what is it all worth?

There's litter on the floor
And there's litter on the shore,
The bins and dumps are about to *pop!*
So, I think it's time to *stop!*

Georgia Tranter (13)
Evesham High School

Our Environment

The grass is no longer green
This world is being ruined
We are not keeping this world clean
This world is coming to an end

Yesterday the sun was beaming
Today is torrential rain
This Earth has stopped gleaming
We keep hurting this planet . . .
Again and again and again

We've got to stop hurting
Our beautiful Earth
We should all be converting
For all it's worth.

Beth Wilkinson (13)
Evesham High School

What's Happening?

What's happening to our home?
Where's all the clean air gone?
Why can't we change our tone?
We did have clean, now we have none.

What's happening to their home?
Why are we causing them pain?
Should we stop destroying their trees?
What are we to gain?

What's happening to our home?
What about the heat?
Can we stop this rising?
We used to be so neat.

What's happening to their home?
Why are they dying?
Can't we stop crushing their home?
It's the ones that are flying.

Lauren Colledge (13)
Evesham High School

Reality

Will we realise,
Will we come to our senses?
The Earth is dying.

We live for our sake,
While Earth is trying to help us,
To see what we have done.

Look around yourself,
We live to nurture not kill,
Start choosing your side.

Darker and darker,
Earth will die as will the time,
We had decided.

Dmitrijs Procs (14)
Evesham High School

I Give You . . . You Give Me . . .

I give you love
You give me war,
I give you life
You give me death.

I give you clean air
You give me pollution,
I give you light
You give me darkness.

I give you clean land
You give me litter,
I give you fields
You give me floods.

I give you happy
You give me sad,
I give you love
You give me heartbreak.

Shannon Silverthorne (13)
Evesham High School

The Earth Is A Marble

The Earth is a marble
Always rolling, always spinning
But when will it stop?

Kids playing marbles
Trading them all day
Thoughtless of what they're trading

A girl on a bench
Is studying her marble
What is she thinking?

Marbles are precious
Just like the Earth and its time
Is that time near?

James Waterhouse (13)
Evesham High School

Goodbye Earth

Earthquakes, landslides, acid rain
Hear our world scream in pain
Monsoons, tsunamis, tidal waves
We are the owner's, the planet's are slaves
Recycle, recycle, recycle once more
Or watch the pollution wash ashore
We spent all our time trying to survive
Thanks to us, the planet isn't alive

All the animals we eat and kill
Is making our world feel ill
The ice caps are melting because of us
That's what's causing all the fuss
We know who to blame, if we're going to die
We will say you, but you would only lie
So, stop pollution, it's bad and foul
All the animals aren't on the prowl.

Connor Gurney (13)
Evesham High School

Litter

Don't be harsh, be green,
Just bin it
Don't be mean,
Just bin it
Look at our world, it is dying out,
Just bin it
Without a doubt,
Just bin it
It needs respect,
Just bin it
We just need to reflect
Just bin it
Don't be cruel, be cool,
Just bin it
Don't litter our planet
Just bin it!

Sam Archer (13)
Evesham High School

The World

I'm in this world to do something
That's what I'm saying
I know that something has to change

Why do we use cars anyway?
I wish I could wish them away
I know that everyone has to change

The world is on fire
That's why God is a liar
I know that we can change

In this world we will die
Unless the weather gives up and cries
I know that me, you, us and everyone
Can change the . . .

World!

Liam West (13)
Evesham High School

Our Environment

Recycle litter
It's destroying the planet
We all need to live

Do not use the cars
Please use those things we call feet
Cars pollute the air

Save our rainforest
Do not cut down those poor trees
We need oxygen

Please use more candles
Don't waste electricity
Think global warming.

Harley Grantham (13)
Evesham High School

Giving It Back

I give you life
You give me death
I give you water
You give me fire

I give you protection
You give me danger
I give you animals
You give me hunting

I give you time
You take it away
I give you water
You give me floods.

Kristian Roberts (13)
Evesham High School

What Have We Done?

What have we done to this world?
How can we fix this world?
How do we stop pollution?
How do we stop global warming?

We must change our ways,
We must change them now,
If we don't change them now,
It will be too late for our world.

The world needs our help,
So help it now,
Before it's too late,
So give up all this prejudice and hate.

Teejay Robbins (13)
Evesham High School

Earth With A Broken Heart

Look at your lovely home
What have we done to it?
Our planet is burning
Can you extinguish that fire?

We are responsible for the broken Earth
We should take care of her
Help your mother
Don't litter your nature

Why don't you eat carrots
Instead of crisps?
You can economize another poison to her heart
And her stomach will be healthier.

Loretta Rybica (13)
Evesham High School

Our World

The world is dying
We need to keep it alive
The world is crying
So why do we seem not to mind?

The world is in our hands
It needs all our respect
We should love and care for each other
So take time out to reflect.

We need to recycle, we need to reuse
We need to cycle and not litter
Help save our planet, there is no excuse
Try and stop our future from being too bitter.

George Hawkins (13)
Evesham High School

The World Is . . .

The world is a set of scales
Very, very unbalanced
The world is in our hands
So why don't we keep it balanced?

The world is an old granny
Growing older every day
Why don't we keep it tidy
And respect it in every way?

The world is a greenhouse
Getting very hot
We need to change our ways
So we don't lose the whole lot.

Alice Hancock (13)
Evesham High School

In Return For Beauty

I gave you hot summers
You give me flooding rivers
I gave you sparkling blue seas
You give me brown, polluted streams

I gave you beautiful swaying trees
You give me lots of wasted paper
I gave you clean, spotless streets
You give me smoky skies

I gave you clean air
You give me acid rain
I gave you sunny seasons
You give me global warming.

Samantha Thomas (13)
Evesham High School

Remember

Remember the time when we used to see
Lush meadows and green grass?
All that's left are landfills full of cans
And broken glass.
Why was nothing ever done? Why did no one see;
That all this mess would come at a price
And nothing would be free?

Remember the time when we used to smell
The fresh flowers you used to like?
Now we all choke on tainted air, because people
Chose car over bike.
Why was nothing ever done? Why did no one see;
That all this mess would come at a price
And nothing would be free?

Remember the time when we used to hear
Trees rustling and birds tweet?
Now, when I listen, I can't hear a thing
Apart from cars along the street.
Why was nothing ever done? Why did no one see;
That all this mess would come at a price
And nothing would be free?

Remember the time when we'd lie down at night
And see the stars in the sky?
Only thing left now is a hazy fog
Which prevents our dreams to fly.
Why was nothing ever done? Why did no one see;
That all this mess would come at a price
And nothing would be free?

Remember the time when people took things for granted
And thought it would last forever?
Now they are seeing things properly for the first time
And have realised that they weren't so clever.

It's too late now to look at one another
And at your polluted planet

If only one person and stood up and asked . . .

'Something needs to be done, can no one else see;
That all this mess will come at a price
And nothing will be free?'

Because if I could go back and warn you all
Of what our world would become
You would all stop and tell yourselves . . .

'Don't act too late
Don't hesitate
Something needs to be done!'

Bronwyn Parton (14)
Madeley Academy

What About The Creatures?

Imagine in your future
Think about your child
Do you think they could ever see
A tiger in the wild?
Give it another fifty years
We will end up in tears
When we lose the last bear
Life is just not fair

Look into your present
See all the creatures
Admire all their beauty
With their different features
Do you prefer a donkey?
Or do you prefer a monkey?
All their numbers are becoming low
One day, they will all go

Remember the past
Some creatures just didn't last
What happened to the dodo?
All God's work has been wasted
The creature was probably not the best
But they went , so could the rest
Save the animals right now
And don't be a cow.

Thomas Morris (13)
Madeley Academy

Killer?

How many animals need to die for us to realise that
               we are killing the world?
How many more icecaps need to melt for us to realise
               we are killing the world?
How much more pollution do we need for us to realise
               we are killing the world?
Do you want to live in a dead world?

How many people need to die due to poverty for us to realise
               we are killing the world?
How many landfill sites do there need to be for us to realise
               we are killing the world?
How many wars do there need to be for us to realise
               we are killing the world?
Do you want to live in a dead world?

How many crimes need to be committed for us to realise
               we are killing the world?
How many habitats need to be ruined for us to realise
               we are killing the world?
How much acid rain does there need to be for us to realise
               we are killing the world?
Do you want to live in a dead world?

By leaving a TV on standby, *you* are killing the world
By leaving a games console on, *you* are killing the world
By leaving a lamp or light on, *you* are killing the world
You are killing the world
But *you* can change this

Turn televisions off at the switch
Turn off your games console when you're finished
Turn off lights when they're not in use
After all, do you want to murder the planet?

Melissa Williams (14)
Madeley Academy

Poverty

Have you ever thought about children in Third World countries?
Have you ever thought about how they feel?
Have you ever thought about what they go through?
Think!
It's time to take action!
When will this stop?
Waiting for someone to come and feed them
Waiting for their sorrow to disappear
This is what children in Third World countries go through
Think!
When will this stop?
No hope for the future
No hope of being fed
No hope of being saved
This is what children from Third World countries feel
Stop!
Think!
Help!
When will all this stop?

Payaal Bhesania (14)
Madeley Academy

If Only

The Earth sheds a tear
It has done nothing wrong by us
If only we could hear
The crying that it does.

The Earth chokes on grime
From pollution and CO_2
If only we could turn back time
And start our world from new.

The Earth won't last forever
Make changes, it's not too late
If only we could endeavour
After all, the Earth's our mate!

Danielle Buxton (14)
Madeley Academy

Outside My Window

I look out of my window and see what we've created
I see people who thought global warming was overrated
I see rivers, once clean, now a gungy paste
And within floats packages, wrappers and waste
I see the dusty blue sheet that I call 'the sky'
I see the remains of smoke from cars passing by

I will look out of my window a year from today
I see the people who know global warming will stay
I see rivers no more, just a dry hole in the ground
And within lurks the litter people have thrown around
I see a dusty grey sheet, that will be smoke from cars
There is no more sky and now, no more stars

I used to look out of my window when I was small
I saw people who'd never heard of global warming at all
I saw rivers fully flowing, never running thin
And the litter and waste was placed in a bin
The crystal-clear sky, the gleaming sun
It was never nature's fault, it's what we have done.

Lucy Thomas
Madeley Academy

War

Welcome to the trenches,
Look at the men in pain,
Fixing things with wrenches,
What do you actually gain?

The opposition is so inhumane,
Destroying everything they see,
It's driving the soldiers insane,
Normal they would like to be!

Families shattered, torn apart
Lives so precious and rare!
Life's a broken heart,
Please, show you care!

Katie Smith (13)
Madeley Academy

What About?

What about soldiers?
What about death?
What about all the pain,
Left for all the people to go insane?

What about weapons?
What about blood?
What about the murder
Left for people to go and cry?

What about the families left all upset?
What about the danger to all of the other people?
What about lives at risk
Taken into hands?

So, please stop the war,
For all of our sakes,
Take it to the door,
To show it the way.

Georgina Skitt (11)
Madeley Academy

Homeless People

H omeless people are all
O n their own with no one to love, not even their
M other, they are cold and frozen
E very day with only the sun and streetlamps to give them
L ight and warmth
E veryone laughs at them, but
S omeone feels
S orry for them

P erhaps they can make a difference and help
E veryone
O f those homeless
P eople, maybe they can change their
L ives, please help make a difference
E ven you could change someone's life forever.

Thomas Price (13)
Madeley Academy

War

Here are the trenches
Lots of men in pain
They're all missing the old park benches
Some won't ever see them again.

Bombs flying in the air
Find somewhere for cover
Men see death at which they stare
Start to miss their lover.

If you saw the end result
War would never start
It would be no one's fault
Everyone would have a working heart.

What is war actually for?
All it causes is death
What is war actually for?
Men taking their last breath.

Carl Davies (13)
Madeley Academy

War + End = Peace

Bang! Bang! A man down
The battlefield full of ecstasy
Poor fearful hostage, safe and sound
Stop now, stop all this fantasy.

Soldiers going through hurtful pain
Men flying head over heels
Why war? What do you gain?
Trucks sliding with burst and tortured wheels.

Rivers and lakes furiously flood
Trees and plants burnt to the top
This is because of the overflow of blood
Stop this now, please stop this now.

Stop! Stop! Stop!

Sagar Jeram (13)
Madeley Academy

This Is The World

This is the world today
Litter flying above and away
Garbage running out of room
Global warming approaching soon
So stop your car and take a walk
Homeless people sit under the moon
You can help and share some room
Rainforests are being cut down
Stop and think about the life
Wars are being run by clowns
Lives are being unnecessarily lost
Black and white seem not to be alike
Even though we're the same
Animals are losing life
While they disappear at night
We all can help and make it right.

Nathaniel Butler (13)
Madeley Academy

Recycle It

It's a disgrace to the human race!
The plastic on the floor, will stay for evermore.
Why couldn't you recycle it?
But instead, you dump it in a pit!

It's a disgrace to the human race!
The can, it's over there by that decomposing pear.
Why couldn't you recycle it?
But *no!* you dump it in a pit!

It's a disgrace to the human race!
That bit of paper on the ground
It will stay there, without a sound
Why couldn't you recycle it?
But once again, you dump it in a stupid pit!

Keeley Summers (13)
Madeley Academy

Recycle To Save

R educe your footprint
E xploit what you get
C hange your lifestyle by recycling
Y ou can change it
C arbon emissions killing more and more
L eaving a footprint every time
E xploit what you get

T aking more and more, giving nothing back
O zone layer repeating holes

S ave the Earth
A ct on your actions
V icious polluting air
E xploit what you get.

Melissa Perry (13)
Madeley Academy

Here I Stand

Here I stand, acid rain falling down
Once happy statues erode into a frown.

Here I stand, mountains and waters frozen
Now melting away because of methods we've chosen.

Here I stand, surrounded by desert and elephants
Now lay skinned because of the rich's demands and wants.

Here I stand, there are trees, creatures running free
Trees now reformed into the paper in front of me.

Why must we do all this?
Put the world through so much pain . . .
When, in the end
There'll be nothing we will gain.

Hannah Sadler (14)
Madeley Academy

War

War is dreadful, so much pain,
Does anyone even care?
What have we got to gain?
Gambling with life so precious and rare.

Think of all the people dying,
Wounded on the battlefield,
Think of all the people crying,
Carrying the memories they shield.

So many families torn apart,
Tortured and scared,
How to mend a broken heart?
No one ever cared.

Yasmin Lavery (13)
Madeley Academy

Save The Penguins

Where it's really, really cold,
The penguins are dying,
Nothing to eat,
While elsewhere, their fish are frying.

Where it's really, really cold,
The penguins are freezing,
We all have our heat,
But it can't be that pleasing.

Where it's really, really cold,
The penguins are innocent,
So we need to help,
Fast!

Suzanne Hopkins (13)
Madeley Academy

War

If people didn't fight
They would have a good night
Parents are dying
Children and babies crying.

If people didn't fight
There would be a lovely sight
With quiet beautiful places
And smiling, happy faces.

If people didn't fight
The end of the tunnel would be light
Everyone would smile
And be willing to walk that extra mile.

Corey Newell (11)
Madeley Academy

Big Green Poetry Machine

Racism is all around us,
On the streets and on the bus,
People don't realise how much it hurts
And out of their mouths it just blurts.

Many people try to hide,
The pain that they have inside,
Just because they're a different race,
I think that it's a disgrace.

People get hurt every day,
From people talking in this way,
But if we all can try,
Racism, we can kiss goodbye!

Jake Lloyd (14)
Madeley Academy

War Games

Welcome to the desert,
We're fighting the Taliban,
Soldiers taking cover,
Their blood is on our hands.

What's war good for,
Apart from reputation?
The state this country's in,
We're begging for salvation.

Look at the damage we've caused,
Look at what we've done,
Flying out to the desert,
Time to cock your gun . . .

Jack Swales (13)
Madeley Academy

War Of The Wilds

War could be beaten if we just tried,
We asked the English government, but they just sighed.
Trenches are filled with guts and blood,
They just all seem like a giant flood.
With bullets flying everywhere,
The British just shoot duck and swear.
Everyone in the world is hoping for peace,
But terrorists and the Taliban are all we seem to seize.
All we are asking for, is a bit of cooperation,
While we try to try to skip the war with our concentrations.
So please, ask for peace and don't doubt,
Or you might see Britain's population wiped out.

Paul Marsh (13)
Madeley Academy

Poem About Recycling

We are very wasteful
This is not very tasteful
We make the acid rain
And it's everyone to blame
I've got a big car
But I only use it when I travel far
Give out the bikes
Give out the trikes
Lose the planes
And the country lanes
Stop the pollution
That's my resolution!

Elliot Stamp (13)
Madeley Academy

Save Our Animals

Lions are running out,
Poachers catch them, raise their cubs,
Foxes, elephants, badgers too,
Everything, including me and you,
Habitats empty,
People destroying them
Foxes, elephants, badgers too,
Everything, including me and you,
Endangered animals,
All gone away forever,
Foxes, elephants, badgers too,
Everything, including me and you.

Amber Willis (12)
Madeley Academy

Hanging By A Thread

In the countries, in the towns
The forests have been cut down
Think, we could stop it
The world's hanging by a thread

Let's use both sides of paper
And save the trees instead

Some countries are spreading disease
So just stop it, please, please, please
Don't cut the thread
That's holding our planet
Please, just save it!

Janie May Richardson (11)
Madeley Academy

I Had A Dream

Like Martin Luther King would say,
I had a dream yesterday,
Floods, fires, sirens galore,
CO_2 affecting more than ever before.

I had a dream
The disasters would end
And make this world a better friend,
Save this world and the entire race,
Please help clean this beautiful place,
End it now, stop all the abuse,
Recycle, think, reuse, reduce!

Jessica-Paris Stokes (13)
Madeley Academy

Save The World

Look at the news
The world is dying
And all the hippies are crying
Love the Earth and don't hate it
Help save it and recycle more
By now is the time
To stop committing the crime
And start preventing acid rain
Because it's a pain
So save the world
Because it gave us everything.

Brad Errock (14)
Madeley Academy

Saving The World

What have we done to the world?
What about the poor, poor animals that are getting killed?
Protect the poor, poor animals
What about the forests that are getting chopped down all the time?
We are the problem
What about the trees?
Recycling paper will help them loads
Please recycle, we need trees to live
What about arson?
Stop burning things and keep the world at peace
Stop and think!

Cara Boden (13)
Madeley Academy

Change Your Way!

Walk to school, don't use the car
Recycle your stuff and stop the war
Pollution is getting worse and worse
It's travelling all across the Earth
It's killing off the woodlands and lakes
Your kids won't see the polar bear race
Instead of throwing away plastic and tins
Place them in your recycling bins
You're killing the planet day by day
So stop now and change your way!

Hazel Flanigan (13)
Madeley Academy

Poverty!

Poverty happens throughout the world,
It happens to all the boys and girls.

Over in Africa and in Brazil,
They get diseases and have to take pills.

We need to raise money, with Children in Need,
But after all the stories, they still chop down trees.

People in poverty, it's not our fault,
But we will try our best to save your souls.

Kellie Pooler (11)
Madeley Academy

You Give Us . . .

You give us llamas
We pollute the air to get to the Bahamas

You give us snakes
We dirty the lakes

You give us sheep
We waste paper to make books like Little Bo Peep

All we do is take
And make lots of wrappers for Flakes.

Nicole Holyhead (13)
Madeley Academy

Pollution

P ollution
O ver the top
L ives ended
L ives sacrificed
U seful cars, but so polluted
T oo many cars on the road
I ncidents caused
O ceans ruined
N o one can stop it now - it has happened.

Kayleigh Harris (11)
Madeley Academy

Untitled

What about stopping crime?
What about stopping pollution?
What about stopping cruelty to animals?
What about stopping war?
What about stopping using plastic?

What have we done to the world?

Shane Howells (13)
Madeley Academy

Untitled

Like a celebration of death
Like a dam of light
That blocks out the sun of hope.

War is Hell
Where people fall into the never-ending abyss
Of darkness.

We must fight the darkness
We must stop the fight.

Daniel Bushell (13)
Madeley Academy

The World

What have we done to the world?
What about stopping crime all around the world?
What about stopping pollution in your cars all around the world?
What about the fact that we should recycle paper all around the world?
What about stopping using plastic all around the world?
What about planting more trees for the animals around the world?
What have we done to the world?

Ryan Barnes (13)
Madeley Academy

The World's Not The Same

This is polluted
This acid rain
Dirty rivers
It's all the same
This ain't a game
So stop making waste
Because you're to blame
The world's not the same!

Will Tinsley (13)
Madeley Academy

What About . . .

What about war when people are hurt?
What about weapons which are used to kill?
What about death when people die?
What about battles when people fight?
What about blood which is on the floor?
What about disaster when something's destroyed?
What about peace when the world rests?

Jessica Smith (11)
Madeley Academy

What About The World?

A nimals are living in fear
N ature is dying
I guanas, pandas and llamas, only a few left
M ost animal species are endangered
A round the world people are dying
L ives are being lost
S o, what are you going to do?

Ravi Bhatia (11)
Madeley Academy

War

Some wars are about politics
Stop all this conflict
Take back all the blood and tears
It's alright to have religion here
Let's not have war
It's not what we're here for.

Thomas Hudson (12)
Madeley Academy

This Is Your World

Creatures from the north belittled,
By towering ice sculptures,
Imprisoned,
The wise, these young,
White soldiers.

Churches suffocated,
By deep, brown waters,
Licking with evil glee,
At the still cherished,
Stained glass windows.

Nothing for miles, the dead lie,
To rot for eternity,
Undergoing despair, longing, hoping
And forever waiting for the pain to end.

White bears, strong like bridges,
But on the run, from a demon,
Mother Nature,
Kind, beautiful, harsh and deadly.

Children crawling in the dust,
Death snatching at their heels,
Waiting for them to grow weaker,
By the day.

Children stalked by vultures,
Waiting for them to fall,
Death, children, extinction,
This is the world you're in.

But the world is changing,
Happiness is spreading,
From each corner of the world,
We are coming, out of the darkness.

Flowers are growing,
Children stopped weeping,
For us, time to rejoice,
A new beginning;
This is your world.

Emily Morris (12)
Mary Webb School

I Wish I Could Fly

Am I flying or am I falling?
Is that a bomb in the sky?
Oh, I wish, I could fly,
Fly away from the bombs,
Fly away from the tournament,
Fly, fly away,
Far, far away now.

It is like a nightmare,
A never-ending nightmare,
Oh, I wish I could fly,
Fly away from this dream,
This never-ending dream,
Oh, I wish I could fly.

The homeless people
Wandering on the streets,
Homeless, helpless,
A bomb is falling,
I can see the German fleets,
Killing and firing guns,
There is not much food,
Only crumbs,
What can we eat?

This war seems never-ending,
I hope we win,
I hope we win to end this tournament,
I wish this war would end,
Oh, how I wish I could fly.

Lauren Dudley (11)
Mary Webb School

Poverty

I'm wet, freezing, I'm starving,
All the food is going,
I've got no shelter,
I've got no hope,
My family are dead
And I'm going
The same way too.

All the animals are dying,
All the houses are falling,
I've got no shelter,
No hope,
Everything is dying,
Even me,
We're all starving
To death.

Why isn't anyone helping us, helping me?
Why isn't anyone coming to my aid?
I'm starving to death
And the flood is getting worse,
It's now as deep as the sea,
All the houses are falling,
Because of it,
Can something be done?

Beth Chandler (11)
Mary Webb School

Pollution

Pollution is bad,
Why can't people see?
It makes me very sad,
Nobody does it to me.

Animals die every day,
Covered in oil from the sea,
They die in every single way,
I'm so glad that's not me.

Molly Jones (11)
Mary Webb School

The Real Issue

Our world turned into a world of water,
Me, you and the animals,
Everything *gone!*
Think of you,
Think of us and everything we've worked for,
Cruel?
Harsh?
Unfair?

This could be our ending,
Speak for those who can't,
Whilst we still have a chance,
The animals do no harm,
Why should they suffer?
It's like building a boat that you know will sink.

This is real life with real problems and real suffering,
How did this happen, so fast, so soon?
Even our cars will leave a scar on global warming,
All work gone to waste,
A real reason to have an unhappy face,
Unfair,
Cruel,
Selfish.

Kirsty Swain (12)
Mary Webb School

Alone

Homeless kids wandering round on the street all alone
No one there to hug or care but a tatty rug on the floor
Bony feet, bony hands
Nothing to wear at all, just a dirty rag on the floor
No food or drink, nothing at all
Just a tired, old rag on the floor
Sitting, staring, mourning, helpless
Hoping for something to happen
Where is the love and affection?

Abigail Bridge (12)
Mary Webb School

Save Our World

The world screams out as it's slowly smothered
A cloud of pollution weighing it down,
The factories function well
Will the world have to write its will?

The patchwork fields are littered
With houses and factories,
Farms just a fading memory,
The animals gone.

Roads now ploughed into the land,
The cars cough and splutter through our towns
Leaving us to slowly suffocate
On their fumes.

Graveyards of washing machines and televisions
Rise from the ground,
Nobody cares, they just want new,
Where has the colour gone?
Everything is gloomy and grey.

Mountains of food wasted,
While children in Africa starve,
Are we all too busy to notice?
Is it too late to save our world?

Harry Game (11)
Mary Webb School

Pollution Is Killing Our Planet

Pollution is killing our planet
Smoke fills the sky
Waste pours into our seas
Pollution is destroying ice in the North Pole
So I made this poem up to stop pollution
Pollution is killing our planet
So maybe we should change the world
Into a better, greener place.

Gareth Goddard (12)
Mary Webb School

Pollution Poem

The chimneys are polluting
What can we do to help?
Well . . .
Solar panels are everywhere,

Wind turbines in the sea,
Come on, Gordon Brown,
This is a major catastrophe,

So if we made our MEC,
Main Energy Convertor
And turn down the temperature
On washing machines,
We can solve our catastrophe,

The ozone layer is burning up,
All of us could die,
The icebergs are melting
And making the sea level rise,

If we all help,
Then maybe we'll win
And fight the major catastrophe!

Jack Johnson (12)
Mary Webb School

Our World Today

Starvation - there are people starving all over the world
There are people stranded as their houses are flooded
They don't have much hope of surviving
Children are on their hands and knees hunting for food
They are poor and there is too much heat around them
Even the animals are finding it hard to survive
There is no water left for them to drink
All the pollution that we are making is making the heat rise
It's melting the icebergs and leaving the polar bears stranded
They have nowhere to go and nothing to eat
It's all down to pollution.

Abigail Leech (11)
Mary Webb School

130

This Is Our World

The devastation of extremes,
The corpses of the dead,
The downpour of pollution,
Foggy skies,
Smoke in the air,
A whole world on fire,
A spotless world, burning.

The quiet despair,
As thin as bones,
Living the animals,
Scorching sun on their bare backs,
Staring, waiting, hoping . . .
An ideal world, starving.

Leaping for their life,
Beauty in disaster,
Drought and deluge,
Desperation over the dead,
A perfect world, melting.

Rachel Harrison (12)
Mary Webb School

What Happens In Our Life

There are loads of children and adults
That die from hunger and drinking dirty water
You can tell by their faces that they are working very hard
To find food for their children and animals
With no animals, there's no food
No food, children and adults will die
There are loads of people whose homes
Get damaged by floods
They can't do anything about it
Every year, floods damage homes
That take years to repair back to normal
Why let this happen to people and children
Who don't deserve it?

Shannon Hughes (12)
Mary Webb School

131

Danger Around The World

Polar bear stranded,
Icebergs coming into hot countries,
Rain pouring all around us,
Cold summers, hot winters.

Parents can't get food for their young,
Food dying like fish from polluted seas,
No one to help people in need from all of the flooding,
Devastation, pollution, unhappiness, starvation.

All the temperature is, is mostly cold and never hot,
Weather changing all the time,
Snow to sun and sun to rain,
Factories polluting the ozone layer.

Recycling is helpful, better than litter everywhere,
It's your fault the world is bad,
Don't forget, there are people in need,
They have no clothes, no food, no water, no home.

Save the world!

Rhianna Reynolds (11)
Mary Webb School

Please Help The World

The Earth is as dark as the Antarctic Sea
This extreme world is coming to meltdown
The poor people living in Africa are so ill, but why?
Why can't we help them?
People are stuck with no food or water to drink
They don't even know what to do or when they will die
How can we help them?
How can we help humans and animals live?
The world cries out for help because they're cold, lonely
Still and stuck and they don't have anyone
They just try to get on with their lives
By finding food and water, trying to survive
So please, how can we help them?

Lydia Goodwin (11)
Mary Webb School

The Slaughter Of Paradise

The world, a hot plate
Extreme drought and deluge at the same time

The rain comes down like a thick mist
Floods carry away our happiness on a swift current

A polar bear, stranded on melting ice, unable to get home
A dad, a son, a cow, all dying
The son asks, 'What is rain?'

A factory fire lights a polluted, orange sky
Thousands of dead fish, polluted, inedible.

A sick and dying bull, someone's last hope
Children look out at you, despair written all over their faces so young.

Pain and suffering circle their bodies, their faces, their eyes
As they scrabble in the dirt for food.

A boy, so still, because of us . . .

Hannah Mai Peacock (11)
Mary Webb School

Is This Fair?

Think of how good your life is
With your warm home and cosy beds
Then think about people that are cold and dying
Gasping for air, is that really fair?

Now think of animals with homes to live in
People to solve their troubles
Now think of polar bears suffering, slowly dying
And the icebergs, their homes, melting.

Now think of how this began
The answer is us!
If we don't change our ways
Who knows what will happen?

Sinead Mulloch (11)
Mary Webb School

The Suffering Earth

People caused the Earth to suffer,
Now people are suffering,
People are dying, starving and miserable,
Waiting, longing, hoping, praying.

Dead fish float on a polluted sea,
An ugly view stretching to the horizon and beyond,
Floods devastate fields, houses and lives,
Death, destruction, misery, illness.

Factories belch out evil smoke,
Polluting the sky for miles around,
Humans brought this on the Earth,
Pollution, crying, lost lives, disintegrating families.

Rescue our poor planet,
It's still not too late,
Humans can stop it
Reuse, recycle, rethink, eco-friendly.

Lauren Forwood (12)
Mary Webb School

Untitled

All the countries and continents
Shine up so bright in the night sky orbit
So why don't they stop and turn the lights off?

Most are suffering from pollution
So why, oh why, didn't we turn the lights off?

Sometime we will all suffer
So why, oh why, oh why, didn't we turn the lights off?

It's as simple as a tick, a flick, a push or a press
So please, turn the light off
You must, you should, or forever dread
The consequences of pollution above your head.

James Ryder (12)
Mary Webb School

Unthinkable, Unwantable

Dying,
Drought,
Starving,
No water spout,
Unthinkable,
Unwantable.

Devastation in the world,
That we didn't even know about,
Unthinkable,
Unwantable.

Sadness in their eyes,
No one to sing them lullabies,
Loved ones dying every day,
Devastation they cry,
Unthinkable,
Unwantable.

Kate Davies (12)
Mary Webb School

Who Do We Blame?

Dirty air, bugs dead
And animals gone for good,
Now people are going hungry
Please give food.

Everything's changing, it's not the same,
I bet you're wondering who's to blame,
Turn to look in a mirror,
Do you see something familiar?

The ozone layer melts away
And soon we'll have to pay.

Everything's changing, it's not the same,
I bet you're wondering who's to blame,
Turn to look in a mirror,
Do you see something familiar . . . ?

Katie Davies (11)
Mary Webb School

Rebuilding Destroyed Lives

Devastation covers the Earth
Like a large, black blanket
Desperate animals and people lying
Amongst dust and death
People freezing with nothing to warm them.

We take for granted what we have
But it is hard not to
So think of them, the starving, the dying
And hope and dream for them.

We can help them if we try
And then they can keep the dream going
That one day the devastation will disappear
So give them some hope and some love
So they have a chance of a better future
Problems are manmade
So Man can fix them.

Kyra Jade Ford (11)
Mary Webb School

Suffer For Hope

Suffering is death
Death comes from suffering
Turn suffering into hope
Hope comes from suffering
Suffering results
In never-ending happiness
By experiencing pain
The world becomes a chain
My world is slowly destroyed
But make an effort
And suffering becomes hope
Hope heals eternity!

Oliver Ansell (11)
Mary Webb School

Heartache

What pain lies behind those heart-aching eyes?
Famine, starvation and longing
Their blank faces pleading with your heart
In their world to live is to be afraid, hungry, tired and alone
Every day harsh as a bitter frost
Where is the glint of happiness
That's supposed to be in that child's eyes?
Stamped on each time till it's mere dust
Drifting away with the wind.

Pollution, devastation and despair
Standing alone on an icy island
Jumping from ice to ice, like stepping stones
Except it's for its life
Everything disappearing, where is it now?
Is there hope with this world?
They are all waiting.

Clara Finnigan (12)
Mary Webb School

The World We Didn't Know

Destroying
Disturbing
Deathly
And desperate
I stand and watch as slowly
Factory smoke fills the air
Killing animals for clothes
It's just not fair
Landfill sites are overflowing
As crimes go on, it's mind-blowing
Pollution is happening here and now
Cutting down trees, we can't allow
Too much fuel is being used up
People littering, fouling things up
All these things are happening in our world
And we just don't know it.

Lauren Jones (11)
Mary Webb School

Homeless

I'm lonely, stranded, starving
I am hoping someone will help me
Slaving away, so I can survive
It is quite scary and upsetting
What shall I do?
I am shaking to death
Too much dust makes me cough
Why me?
Why my family?
I want a home
Someone come and rescue me
I am starting to disappear
Disappear into thin air
Fading away each day
I take one step
Then . . . I'm *gone!*

Emma Hockly
Mary Webb School

The World's People

Skinny, starving, sad
I stand there and watch
The homeless, starving people die
We can help
But sometimes we don't
We can send some food
Or warm blankets
But we don't
We could waste less food
But we don't
Will someone do something
Or will they just let people die?

Rachael Fortune (12)
Mary Webb School

Into The Dark

Stabbing, death,
These are the things I see,
As knife crime goes on,
Policemen running,
Grabbing the man,
Poor child, lying there,
Bleeding, dying,
Ambulance rushing,
To save the child,
It's too late,
If only I could wave a wand
And it would go away.

Thomas Hopkins (11)
Mary Webb School

I Am The World

I am the world covered in litter
Pollution in the air is making me less fitter
The trees on my body are being cut down
Making the landscape look like a ghost town
My ice caps are melting, making the water level rise
It's happening all the time, just open your eyes
I am slowly dying, it is quite clear to see
It doesn't take much to try and help me
Recycle, reuse and turn the lights out
Try and reuse water to prevent a drought
So help me and clean me and make your work seen
Try to convince other people to go green!

Ewan Grainger (11)
Mary Webb School

What Can We Do?

Our big world is heating up,
Slowly, very slowly,
Ice is melting,
All is silent,
Our big world is heating up.

Black smoke fills the city air,
People choking to death,
The pollution,
Suffocating,
Black smoke fills the city air.

What can we do?

Paige Moore (12)
Mary Webb School

Is The World Spinning?

Animals on the border of surviving
Polar bears stranded
Nowhere to go
Fish dying
Extreme flooding
Snow is melting
Into the cold, icy ocean
Air pollution maximizing
Global warming winning
People starving
Is the world still spinning?

Tanita Morris-Skitt (12)
Mary Webb School

Help!

I'm stranded out at sea,
I'm cold and lonely,
I feel weak,
I'm slowly dying,
We look for help,
Look everywhere,
No one,
Nowhere,
Disappearing into the air,
We're all dying,
Losing our souls.

Sophie Jones (11)
Mary Webb School

Listen Up!

Do you want to be the number one polluter of the world?
Well, listen up . . .
You need to . . .
Reduce, reuse, recycle,
Don't litter,
Think of polar bears and turn lights off,
When you don't need them on,
Walk more and use the car less,
Turn switches off when you aren't using them,
Switch the TV off, instead of using it
And not turning it off!

Holly Hurdley (12)
Mary Webb School

Our World

What are we doing to this world?
Polar bears stranded on ice, like they're trapped in a cage
Furious fish abandoned because of polluted water
What are we doing to this world?
People pleading for help
Adults and children ravenous because of famine
They rely on a good harvest but it never turns out right
What are we doing to this world?
Flooding washes away people's homes and livelihoods
Their lives drown in despair
What are we doing to this world?

Keira Holder (11)
Mary Webb School

No More Knife Crime!

Every day, so many people die
Due to knife crime, it must make you cry
Young boys and girls, adults too
Are being stabbed right out of the blue.

Now, you may think that you can't stop it
But you can help by doing your bit
If you know someone who wants to start
Warn them not to get into that art!

Help the world to stop knife crime
Cos one day a knife might end your time.

Timothy Burns (11)
Mary Webb School

What Do We Gain?

Starving people grasping for life,
Melting icebergs, why . . . ? Because of us!
Flooding, properties ruined, a small price to pay,
War, losing people that we love, what do we gain?
Imagine a foot as big as England
Making a gaping hole in the Earth's atmosphere,
Drought and diseases cover the Earth, like a shower of rain,
Air pollution causing lung diseases, we can't hold our breath,
Water pollution and over-fishing threatens marine life,
Switch off lights and conserve energy for a brighter planet.

Rhys Williams (11)
Mary Webb School

War

Trapped alone, while I see the enemy running towards me
While the bombs shatter and shout down your ear
The enemy firing the bullets, *bang, bang, bang!*
The screams of the soldiers dying
The sound of a tank moving, then suddenly it stops
In front of you, *bang!*
The last thing you hear, your hearing comes back
A sniper in the air, then blackout!
You lower to the ground and see the dead
Then you become one of them.

Liam Caswell (11)
Mary Webb School

Hey Diddle, Diddle

Hey diddle, diddle,
What's that in the middle?
A cow lying dead by the door,
The little child wept to see such pain
And the dish lay bare on the floor.

Jessica Cox (12)
Mary Webb School

The Question Poem

Why do people starve under the midnight stars?
Why do fish die of pollution under the blue blanket?
Why do we have enough food and they don't?
Can we save the animals that live today?
Why do we live in a rich place and they don't?
Why do polar bears lose their land in the North?
How do African people survive?
Why do we learn more than people that live in poor countries?
Why do we live longer than people in Africa?
Why do we have better lives than the dying people in poor countries?

Max Entwistle (11)
Mary Webb School

Why War?

Wandering around the bomb-ridden town I call home
I look everywhere, but just see the corpses
Of my one-time friends, who weren't as lucky as me
Well, I say that, but with nothing to eat
I may be joining them soon
I'm a homeless orphan
All basements taken up by families
Whereas I'm a lonely orphan walking in a graveyard
I'm in a desolate place, that has no hope of recovery
Why, oh why, do we have to have war?

Sarah McMillan (11)
Mary Webb School

Lost Land

Foul furnaces dominate our dirty skyline
Pollution slowly eating away at our battered atmosphere
Ice caps are melting
Sea levels are rising
Low lying land is being reclaimed by the sea.

Thomas Johnson (12)
Mary Webb School

Silver To Red

I'm cold and scared, pain searing through me,
Waiting for them to strike again, *thwack, thwack!*
I feel my ribs crack with each kick that hits my body like a bus,
I open my eyes, I watch the glint of the knife
Slowly turn to red as it sinks in
I'm losing consciousness, the feeling sapping out of me
I hear the sirens, running
And into the *darkness.*

Lily Finnigan (12)
Mary Webb School

Don't Shut The Door

Don't shut the door on people who are poor,
They need your help,
So don't leave them and let them starve,
The world is rough, so we've got to be tough,
We've got to share and be aware
That we can't have it all,
Let's all come together forever,
For the sake of our children and the planet.

Tyler Alcock (11)
Mary Webb School

Why Don't They Listen?

I step outside, into this destroyed world and see people littering
The deforestation is driving me crazy
I can't stand it anymore, watching the world torn apart
Something must be done
I start to run
Shouting out to catch their attention
But yet, I'm still not sure they hear
I'll never give up hope and I'll keep trying.

Connor Sturrock (11)
Mary Webb School

Homeless

There's a man sitting all alone,
With no house and with no home,
He has no food
And not a single room,
He is far too skinny,
So help this man, who's got no home,
Because he still may be sitting alone.

Becci Lewis (11)
Mary Webb School

The Day I Die

Sitting in a room, all cold and with cramp
Struggling to survive
As his room's so damp
Legs all shaky and arms thin and bony
While the rest of the world are happy and cosy
How could you think of a poor, poor man
Sitting in a room all cold and with cramp.

Jack Breeze (11)
Mary Webb School

Litter Poem

Litter is bad
It makes me sad
Please pick it up

Litter is my hate
Just throw it in the bin, mate
When it's on the floor, it's too late.

Jacob Cooper (11)
Mary Webb School

Animal Slaughter

We must stop animal slaughter
We must stop it now!
We must stop killing animals today
If we kill animals, what can we do?
Why can't everyone be vegetarians?
So please, stop it now!

Thomas Beddows (11)
Mary Webb School

Racism

Racism is bad
It makes me feel sad
Colour doesn't matter
Think about what's inside
Some people are horrified
People are doing it worldwide.

Luke Chidley (11)
Mary Webb School

Think

Time is going by, we need to start to think!
Our world is going down and down the sink
We could start to pick up all the litter
Or recycle all the rubbish we put in the bin!
It can't be that hard
We just have to *think!*

Elizabeth Holmes (11)
Mary Webb School

Litter

The ozone layer is getting thin
Please recycle your biscuit tin
Every day we pollute the air
Soon there will be no polar bear
All the streets are more grimy
Day by day the ocean grows slimy.

Elliott Coyne (12)
Mary Webb School

Pollution

Pollution is making the Earth cry,
Knife crime is making people die,
Someday the Earth will go away,
Then it'll make people pay,
The animals and Earth will die,
If we keeping polluting our sky!

Adam Davies (12)
Mary Webb School

Devastation

As the child sleeps, it hopes that when it wakes up
It will have food and a real bed to sleep in
As the sky looks down on Earth, it cries and weeps
For what we have done is unforgiveable
So as the child sleeps and the sky weeps
I wonder, why has this happened?

Jake Elsey (11)
Mary Webb School

What Have We Done?

Volcanoes trembling
Tummies rumbling
Cutting down trees
No more bees
Exploding seas
What have we done?

Jed Delaney (11)
Mary Webb School

The War

The boy was walking home
When he heard a sudden sound,
A building had been set on fire
And hurtled to the ground,
As armed soldiers crowded around,
The boy felt like his world had come,
Crashing down.

The soldiers shoved and pushed him
Out of the way,
He will never be able to forget that day,
His family and all he had ever loved,
Had now left him to go above.

The atmosphere around him
Was filled with pain,
He didn't understand what anyone would gain,
The boy started to flee with tears in his eyes,
He wanted to get away from these hurtful lies.

The fires burnt out as night drew near,
The boy lay in the street
Though no one seemed to care,
His family and all he had ever cared for,
Were now gone . . . because of this stupid war.

Donique Lee (14)
Menzies High School

The Environment

The environment is cool!
Don't mess it up
Pollution is wrong
Although it takes long
The ozone is great
You'll think it's your mate
Natural disasters
You'll need a plaster!

Greenhouse gases
They come in masses
Chopping down trees
You wrecked it for the bees!
Global warming is a sin
Put your litter in a bin!

The environment is cool!
Don't mess it up
This is my warning . . .
Don't mess it up!

James Weston (13)
Menzies High School

Do Something About It!

There are adults and children dying out there
And I'm doing nothing about it
No houses to live in, no cure for their illness
And I'm doing nothing about it
Being used as slaves and beaten to a pulp
And I'm doing nothing about it
Living in poverty with no jobs to earn money
And I'm doing nothing about it
They have enough food a week to last us a day,
No water to hydrate
And I'm doing nothing about it
If we don't do something soon, they will all be gone,
Come on, do something about it!

Rebecca Young (13)
Menzies High School

150

Stop Cutting Trees

Chopping is good for some,
If you think this, you're dumb,
Chopping trees,
Means you're killing bees.

Birds make beautiful nests,
By chopping you become a pest,
Animals cry and cry,
Some also die and die.

Squirrels look for nuts,
Chopping trees give them cuts,
Chopping trees is wrong,
Although it might take long.

Trees are living things,
They're as important as your rings,
Trees give you some air,
That's why you should care.

Stop chopping trees!

Rajinder Singh (13)
Menzies High School

Save The Animals

Animals are wonderful
Giving lots of love
But we need to pull together
And stop extinction
But most of all, we need to stop
Otherwise there will be no cats
There will be no dogs
No tigers, lions and cheetahs
Or elephants, rhinos or hippos
And there will be none
If we don't change
And help more animals
And keep animals in a high range.

Theo Richards (14)
Menzies High School

Filthy Goggles

I stepped out of my house
And suddenly, the world looked different
It was like looking at a table from a weird angle
I got ready to take in oxygen
And made a disgusted face
The polluted air made brown, filthy goggles
And placed them on my face
I tried to take them off
But they wouldn't budge
I didn't want to see how the sea creatures were dying
Because of the junk piled into the sea
I didn't want to see our nature drooping down
Because we've used their body for worthless paper
I didn't want to see our rubbish bins piled to the top
When there are people starving
But I saw it all
Until I couldn't see anything, but the shadows of what remains . . .

Laynah Nathan (13)
Menzies High School

Changes

I look around the world,
What do I see?
I see pain, hunger and poverty,
Shanty towns in Bombay,
Children dying every day.

We need a revolution,
To rid us of pollution,
The world is not blind,
It just doesn't wanna see,
The damage caused by you and me.

Heal the world,
Make it a better place,
For you, for me
And the entire human race!

Tina Sehmar & Beth Walker (14)
Menzies High School

On, Off

Lights, TV, blender
On
Microwave, computer, dryer
On

You would think that's enough
But they keep going on
That's too much, just turn them off
Is it so hard to just use one?
Stop. Breathe. Take a moment and think
Did you turn the water off in the kitchen sink?

Lights, TV, blender
Off
Microwave, computer, dryer
Off
Saving the environment is as simple as that
It is time for this to stop.

Brittany Harrison (14)
Menzies High School

Animals

You may have seen an animal today,
But tomorrow it may not be there,
Animals don't just disappear, you see
They need a lot of care.

Animals are funny creatures,
Each one with different features,
Some with two legs,
Others with four,
Some talk with a voice,
Others talk with a roar.

Animals need us,
To save each race,
What would life be
Without an animal's face . . . ?

Danielle Joseph (14)
Menzies High School

War

War is a bore,
Hear the gunshots roar,
Watch the planes soar,
Dropping bombs, dropping bombs
And nuclear missiles.

War isn't right,
All we do is fight,
No one sees the light,
Guns and tanks, guns and tanks,
Nothing is achieved.

Everyone just dies
And their families cry,
Always wondering why,
They gave their lives, they gave their lives,
To save their own country.

Gari Hardiman (13)
Menzies High School

The Bad News

Bombs . . . yet another . . . death . . . guns . . . *war!*

Even though the signal crackled,
We kind of got the gist,
The world was on the brink of war,
It's always been like this.

Another day, another death,
Another mother on this Earth left,
Crying friends knowing their fate,
A grieving widow in an awful state.

I hate to say, it looks this bad,
But the truth must be told,
I wonder when the end will be?
It's starting to look like World War III.

Bethany Turner (13)
Menzies High School

The Ice Is Melting

It's sad to think,
We're so naïve,
That we don't even realise,
Every day we send pollution,
Up into the skies.

The trees are dying,
They're calling for help,
While the ice is melting
And polar bears yelp.

I look at an ivory sculpture
And wonder which animal died,
Lions are dying out rapidly,
Just a few are left in the pride.

Daniella Lee (14)
Menzies High School

The Environment

E lectricity - turn off the switch
N atural disasters
V ery important to help the environment
I nfinite people wasting resources
R ecycle so there's less rubbish
O zone layer
N o more greenhouse gases
M ake people more eco-friendly
E xtinction must stop
N o more cars giving out gases and smoke
T sunami - wrecking people's homes.

Chelsea Broadmore-Rammell (13)
Menzies High School

The Environment Poem

E arthquakes are not very nice
N either are any natural disasters
V ery many animals are extinct
I f everyone stopped dropping litter and
R ecycled there wouldn't be a problem
O ur ozone layer is getting destroyed by
N atural disasters and
M any different other things, so stop using so much
E nergy around your home and save the
N ature's homes and don't chop trees down
T sunamis can damage our *environment!*

Aaron Crofton (13)
Menzies High School

About The Environment

E nvironments are different places
N o one is thinking about pollution
V ery crowded places
I mportant things such as recycling
R ain, sun, cold, wind, earthquakes, hope they don't come
O il shortages, chopping trees, natural disasters why do they come
N o more tsunamis, bring us all together
M oving onto recycling where people don't care
E veryone could do their bit
N ow greenhouses cause even more gases
T o global warming, which might make problems.

Bethany May Parkes (13)
Menzies High School

Oh, Litter . . .

Every night when I look out of my bedroom window
I see litter on the streets, amongst people's feet
Oh, why can't people see, that
It looks so untidy
And see that rubbish belongs in the bin!
I wish I could just see the tarmac of the streets
And for the park to be tidy without the cans
Hopefully one day
I will look out of my bedroom window
And magically the litter will disappear . . .

Laura Davis (14)
Menzies High School

Sorry's Not Good Enough

I won't stop believing that this is the end,
There must be another way,
Cos I couldn't handle the thought of you going away,
The end can't be near, there's something we must do,
No one would handle there being no you,
Don't stop all those things you do,
I'm a believer and that's what gets you through,
I can't fight this feeling that this is the end,
We're in the thick of it, where will this ever end?

Laura Talbot (13)
Menzies High School

Don't Drop Litter

Don't drop litter,
Litter is a crime,
You might get fined,
So you'd better change your mind,
It's affecting the world today,
So think before you drop it,
That's how people will stop it!

Sophie Louise Parkins (11)
Menzies High School

If It Wasn't For Them

(Dedicated to each and every soldier who fights for their people)

If it wasn't for them,
The brave ones, who put their lives on the line,
Whether they believe the reason is justified,
To them, it makes no difference,
The frightened soldiers on the front line,
There's no rest for them, the war's going on all of the time.

But dodging death comes at a cost,
For every side has to compensate for the lives lost,
Grieving families weep as their beloved ones return,
But no longer in a human form,
Instead, draped in the mighty country's mighty flag.

If it wasn't for them,
The world wouldn't be as we know it,
All independence would be lost, parts of the world wouldn't exist,
Half the world might speak the same language
And we would have no human rights.

Be grateful to them
And show the respect they deserve.

Danny Roberts (14)
The Woodlands School

War!

War, war - what is it for?
War, war - why are we in it?
War, war - for the glory?
War, war - who's gonna win it?

War, war - it's all regret
War, war - we won't forget
War, war - the people who died
War, war - at least they tried

War, war - innocent people
War, war - all over the world
War, war - suicide bombers
War, war - full of hatred and love

War, war - what is it for?
War, war - why are we in it?
War, war - for the glory?
War, war - who's gonna win it?

Luke Bowden (13)
The Woodlands School

Rainforest

A monkey munching on its food
The crash of elephants when they're in a mood
A tiger roaring at its prey
All the animals walking to the bay
All the big, beautiful flowers
And all the wet rain showers
A big brown tree falling
The sound of birds calling
All the animals making a show
An army soldier taking a heavy blow
A butterfly spinning around
An ant coming out of a mound
This is my rainforest poem
Now I am going.

Samuel Jackson (11)
The Woodlands School

159

Global Warming

G reedy people using their cars
L oving environment people trying to help
O bliterating the environment
B attering the ice caps
A reas of sizzling heat
L ittle animals dying in the heat

W arning, warning, the Earth is dying
A ngry, hot and bothered people
R unning, screaming people
M an, don't use your car so much
I cky, horrible heat
N aughty people killing the Earth
G rim people warming the Earth.

Sam Burgwin (11)
The Woodlands School

The Sound Of War

The sound of guns firing,
The sound of people dying,
The sound of enemies at the door,
This is the sound of war.

The charge over the trench,
Backed up by the French,
The black cloak of death,
Loomed over every breath.

Friends dying around you,
Finally I am hit too,
Then I hit the floor,
This was the sound of war.

Rory Parsons (13)
The Woodlands School

War

War takes a huge decision
With guns you need timing and precision
People that die, day after day
Death is a good thing, some people say

Why should we kill?
Every gunshot, blood starts to spill
Some people die, others cry
Everywhere I go, dead bodies lie

War is so terrible, it's horrible and cruel
Dead people everywhere, even in the swimming pool
Finally the war is over, less people die
Still every day, lots of people cry.

Robbie Albrighton (13)
The Woodlands School

The White Tiger

W hite creatures prowl
H unting in disguise
I n their snowy coats
T aking out their prey
E xtinction is near

T hese creatures are not for hunting
I n the wild they roam
G etting killed for trophies
E xtinction is not a virtue
R unning away all the time.

Ethan Hammersley (13)
The Woodlands School

Rainforest

R oots in the ground
A nimals howling happiness
I nsects crawling all around
N obody in sight
F alling leaves
O pen air rushing wind
R oaring lions in the dark
E lephants stomping in the breeze
S ilent monkeys in the trees
T all trees floating in the breeze.

Kurtis Aston (11)
The Woodlands School

What Is War?

Is war good or is it bad?
Why must we fight in Baghdad?
Blood is spilt and lives are lost
Everyone pays at a cost
Families grieve, friends in despair
Over a loved one for whom they care
So is war good or is it bad?
Let's pull our troops out of Baghdad
Away from fear, away from scare
Give everyone rights to make life fair!

James White (13)
The Woodlands School

War

Millions of men standing tall,
One by one they will fall.
Millions of men in a line,
Ready for battle, it starts at nine!

Thousands of guns ready to go,
Hundreds of men they will mow.
A month or two, most will be dead,
War really does mess with your head.

Jack Ranger (13)
The Woodlands School

Boom, Boom

It's a sad thing
People die and kill
Families destroyed
Their lives stand still

Boom, boom, he fires his gun
Boom, boom, he looked at the sun
Boom, boom, then he was blind
He got shot in the head and he was dead.

Luke Essex (13)
The Woodlands School

In It To Win It

War, war, why are we in it?
War, war, why don't they bin it?

War, war, we're fighting and dicing
War, war, we're locking and loading.

War, war, we are in it to win it
War, war, we ain't running until we have won it!

Dominic Palmer (13)
The Woodlands School

War

W ar will never prevail
A t all battlegrounds
R ighteous causes will win

W ar always involves killing
A ll families of those dead are weeping
R ight is wrong in war.

Ryan Gyr (13)
The Woodlands School

Young Writers Information

We hope you have enjoyed reading this book - and that you will continue to enjoy it in the coming years.

If you like reading and writing poetry drop us a line, or give us a call, and we'll send you a free information pack.

Alternatively if you would like to order further copies of this book or any of our other titles, then please give us a call or log onto our website at www.youngwriters.co.uk

Young Writers Information
Remus House
Coltsfoot Drive
Peterborough
PE2 9JX
(01733) 890066